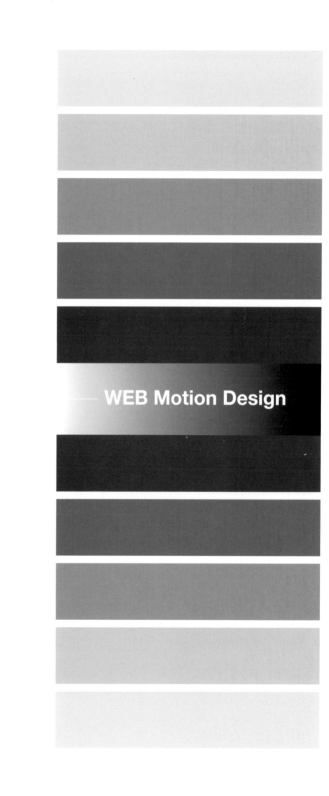

WEB Motion Design

WEB Motion Design

WEB モーション デザイン

P·I·E BOOKS
Villa Phoenix Suite 301, 4-14-6,
Komagome, Toshima-ku, Tokyo 170-0003 Japan
Phone: +81-3-3940-8302 Fax: +81-3-3576-7361

e-mail:
editor@piebooks.com
sales@piebooks.com
http://www.piebooks.com

ISBN4-89444-188-8 C3070

First Published in Germany 2002
by NIPPAN Nippon Shuppan Hanbai Deutschland GmbH
Krefelder Strasse 85, D-40549, Düsseldorf, Germany
Tel:+49-(0)211-5048080 Fax:+49-(0)211-5049326

ISBN3-935814-12-7
Printed in Japan

P·I·E
BOOKS

CONTENTS

Index of
Design Firm

Die Entwicklung der Animation

Gedruckte Bücher und Periodika, Photographie und Film, Fernsehen und das Internet - alle Arten der Medien haben das übergeordnete Ziel, die Aufmerksamkeit des Konsumenten zu gewinnen. Dies kann erreicht werden, indem man die spezifische Dynamik des jeweiligen Mediums vorteilhaft nutzt. Kompositionen mit Bewegung sind immer eindrucksvoller als statische Elemente. Die Evolution hat das Auge des Menschen trainiert, ständig nach sich bewegenden Objekten zu schauen und Veränderungen der Umgebung wahrzunehmen, die ja eine Gefahr sein könnten oder ein Raubtier.

Dieser Instinkt existiert immer noch und macht Animation zu einem sehr effizienten Verfahren, den Betrachter durch die Schlüsselpunkte einer Komposition zu leiten. Animierte Elemente einer Website sind blickfangender und verführen zum Anclicken. Websites mit grauem Hintergrund und blauem Text von Kante zu Kante sind Vergangenheit. Die Webdesigner von heute haben eine breite Werkzeugpalette zur Kreation stimulierender Websites zur Verfügung : von einfachen Überblendungseffekten programmiert mit JavaScript über animierte GIFs zu komplizierten, interaktiven Flash-und Shockwave-

Animationen. Alle diese Techniken beinhalten ein immenses Potential zur Aufwertung einer Website wie aber auch die Gefahr, sie zu überladen und schreierisch zu machen. Diese Werkzeuge haben eine scharfe Klinge und sind ungeeignet für den untalentierten Nachahmer.

Professionelle Webdesigner und Künstler bemühen sich ständig, die Grenzen der Internet-Gestaltung auszuweiten. Sie nutzen die neuesten Techniken, um ihre Ideen zu visualisieren. Da immer mehr Internet-Nutzern die Breitband-Technik zur Verfügung steht, werden wir in der nächsten Zukunft große Veränderungen in der Web-Animation beobachten können. Das Internet der Zukunft wird wahrscheinlich mehr dem Fernsehen ähneln oder den 3D-Computerspielen als dem statischen Buch, bei dem von Seite zu Seite geblättert werden muß. Web-Animation ist im Prozeß der Evolution und nutzt dabei vorteilhaft seine eigene Dynamik.

Reinhard Marscha jr.
EYE4U active media

Evolution of Animation

From printed books and papers, through photography and motion pictures, to television and the Internet, the topmost goal of all types of media has been to catch the consumer's attention. This can be attained by taking advantage of the specific dynamism the media of choice offers: dynamical compositions in still pictures or actual motion in film are more impressive than static elements. Evolution trained the eyes of our ancestors to be constantly on the watch for moving objects and for changes in the environment that might represent danger or a prey.

This instinct is still present, and makes animation highly efficient in guiding the viewer through the key points of a composition, or making animated elements on a Website more catchy and clickable. Websites with grey backgrounds and blue text from border to border are relics of the past.

Today's Web designers and artists are provided with a wide range of tools to create visually stimulating Websites: from simple rollover effects programmed with JavaScript, through animated GIFs, to sophisticated and interactive Flash and Shockwave animations. All of these techniques hold an immense potential for upvalueing your Web design, as well as, unfortunately, for making it too profuse and flamboyant. These tools have blades that are too sharp for the untalented dabbler.

Professional Web designers and artists are permanently pushing the edge of the Internet, using the latest techniques to visualize their ideas. With more and more users on high-bandwidth Internet connections, we will definitely see some big changes in Web animation in the near future. The Internet of the future will probably look more like television or a 3D computer game, rather than a static book, clicking or scrolling from page to page. Web animation is still in the process of evolution — taking advantage of its own dynamism.

Reinhard Marscha jr.
EYE4U active media

EDITORIAL NOTES
クレジットフォーマット CREDIT FORMAT

モーション画像の順番は、ページ内の向かって左から右です。一番右の画像の次は一つ下の段へ下がって、同じように向かって左から右へ流れていきます。　A turn of a motion image in a page go, and is the right from the left. Next of the most right image falls down to a step under one and go in the same way and will drift from the left to the right.

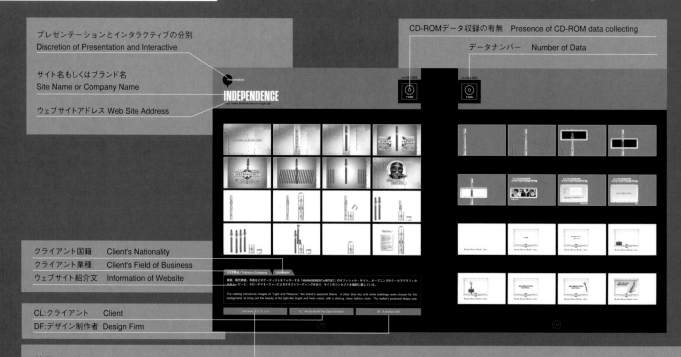

プレゼンテーションとインタラクティブの分別
Discretion of Presentation and Interactive

サイト名もしくはブランド名
Site Name or Company Name

ウェブサイトアドレス Web Site Address

CD-ROMデータ収録の有無　Presence of CD-ROM data collecting

データナンバー　Number of Data

クライアント国籍　　Client's Nationality
クライアント業種　　Client's Field of Business
ウェブサイト紹介文　Information of Website

CL:クライアント　　Client
DF:デザイン制作者　Design Firm

使用ソフトウェア Software use for Designing the Site

- ウェブアニメーション制作ソフト Web Cartoon Film Production Software
  - A　…Flash (Macromedia)
- グラフィック作成ソフト Graphic Making Software
  - B-1 … Illustrator (Adobe Systems)
  - B-2 … Photoshop (Adobe Systems)
  - B-3 … Free Hand (Macromedia)
  - B-4 … Quark Xpress (Quark)
- グラフィック圧縮テクノロジー Graphic Compression Technology
  - C　… Acrobat (Adobe Systems)
- ビデオ編集ソフト Video editing Software
  - D-1 … Premiere (Adobe Systems)
  - D-2 … iMovie (Apple Computer)
  - D-3 … Final Cut Pro (Apple Computer)
- 3Dグラフィック作成ソフト 3D Graphic Making Software
  - E-1 … Light Wave 3D (Newtek)
  - E-2 … Strata Studio Pro (Strata)
  - E-3 … 3d studio max (discreet)
  - E-4 … Swift 3D (Electric Rain)
- 3D人物形成作成ソフト 3D Person Formation Making Software
  - F　… Poser (Curious Labs)
- サウンド編集ソフト Sound Editing Software
  - G-1 … Sound Forge (Sonic Foundry)
  - G-2 … Sound Edit (Macromedia)
  - G-3 … Cooledit 2000 (Syntrillium Software)

- G-4 … Soundhack (Free Software-Tom Erbe作)
- midi&サウンド統合ソフト Midi & Sound Integrated Software
  - H-1 … Cubase UST (cubase)
  - H-2 … Logic Audio (emagic)
- サウンド処理プログラム sound processing program
  - I　… Marcohack
- ソフトシンセサイザー Software Synthesizer
  - J　… Thonk 0+2 (Audio Ease)
- テキストエディタ Text Editor
  - K　… BB Edit (Bave Bones Software)
- ビデオエフェクトソフト Video Effect Software
  - L　… After Effects (Adobe Systems)
- マルチメディアシステム機能拡張 Multimedia INIT
  - M　… Quick Time (Apple Computer)
- マルチメディアオーサリングソフト Multimedia Authoring Software
  - N　… Director (Macromedia)
- マルチメディアファイル圧縮テクノロジー Multimedia File Compression Technology
  - O-1 … Shockwave (Macromedia)
  - O-2 … Media Cleaner Pro (Terran Interactive)
- HTMLエディター HTML Editor
  - P　… Dreamweaver (Macromedia)
- ウェブサイト開発ツール Website Development Tool
  - Q-1 … Generator (Macromedia)
  - Q-2 … Visual InterDev (Microsoft)
- ウェブサイトオーサリングツール Website Authoring Tool
  - R　… GoLive (Adobe Systems)

neopod

http://www.neopod.net

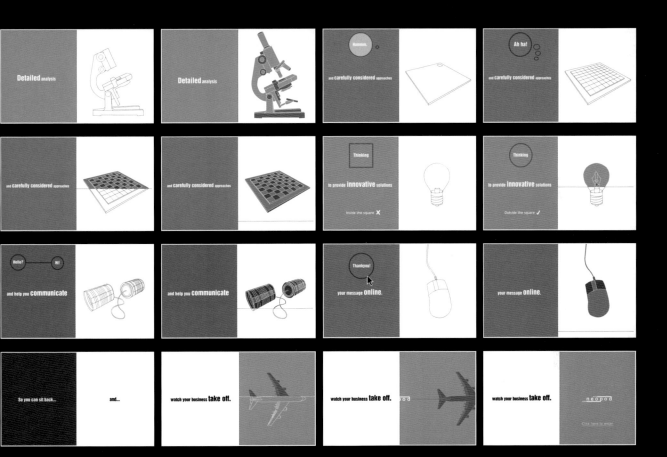

AUSTRALIA / デジタルデザイン／Digital Design

デジタルデザインを手掛ける「Neopod」のサイト。画面左側に表示される言葉に対して、関連のあるイラストが形成され、色付く様子が一定のリズムに合わせて展開されている。抑え気味の色が画面をすっきり、上品に見せている。

Site of "Neopod" handling a digital design. A word displayed on the left of the screen, then an illustration related to the word is formed and colored with constant rhythm. A color bringing under control shows a screen elegantly.

Soft ware : A	CL : Neopod	DF : Neopod

http://www.ikda.co.uk

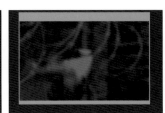

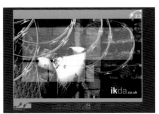

デザイン事務所／Design Studio ▸ UK

紙媒体からインターネット、マルチメディアまで幅広く活動しているデザイン事務所「IKDA Studios.」のサイト。オープニングで現れるオレンジのフレームが効いている。コンテンツを選択すると縦横垂直に動くオレンジのラインが交差しながら白い半透明のボックスを形成していく。

Site of design office "IKDA Studios." where is widely active from a paper medium to Internet, multimedia. It is effective for an orange frame appearing with an opening. Crisscrossing orange lines will form a white semitransparent box when a user select contents.popular among customers.

Soft ware : A, B-1, B-2, D-1, D-2 | CL : IKDA Studios. | DF : IKDA Studios.

neo2

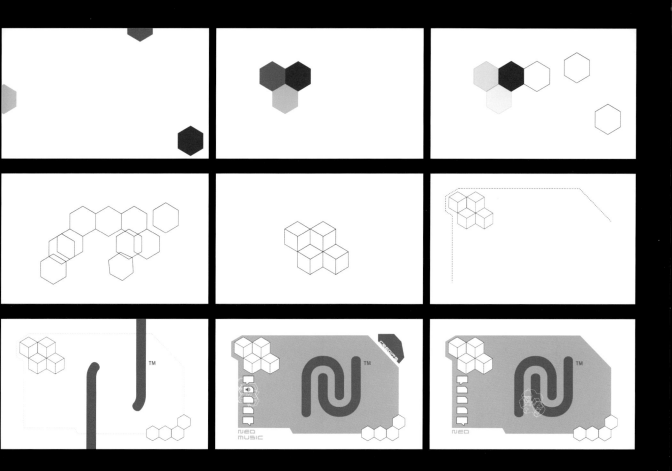

SPAIN グラフィックデザイン事務所／Graphic Design Studio

スペインのデザイン事務所「Ipsum Planet」のサイト。白とブルーを基調としたさわやかなレイアウト。リズミカルなサウンドにのって、ラインアート的なグラフィックスが動き、メニューページを形作っていく。白抜きのライングラフィックスが、カーソルに合わせて形を変化させながら動きまわる。

Site of Spanish design office "Ipsum Planet." It has basic tone and the refreshing layout by using white and blue. With rhythmical sound, graphics of line art changes and will form a menu page. The graphics of white lines moves as it changes its form with a movement of a cursor.

Soft ware : A	CL : Ipsum Planet	DF : xnografics

neostream

http://www.neostream.com

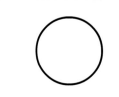

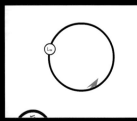
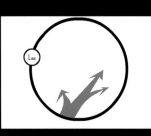

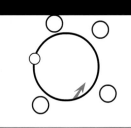

マルチメディア＆ウェブサイトデザイン／Multimedia & Web Design/Development　　**AUSTRALIA**

CD-ROMタイトル、コーポレーション・デザイン、ウェブデザインを手掛けるカンパニー、「Neostream」のオフィシャルサイト。さすが商業デザインの会社だけに、キャッチーでポップな動きが多く、一度目にしただけで印象が強く残る。構造がシンプルなのもいい。

Neostream is a design company that specializes in corporate design, Web design, and creation of CD-ROM titles. Because it is a commercial design company, the site contains a lot of catchy, pop movement, which leaves a strong impression on the first-time viewer. The simple site structure is also nice.

Soft ware : A, B-1, B-2, E-1, G-1, P　　　　CL : Neostream　　　　DF : Neostream

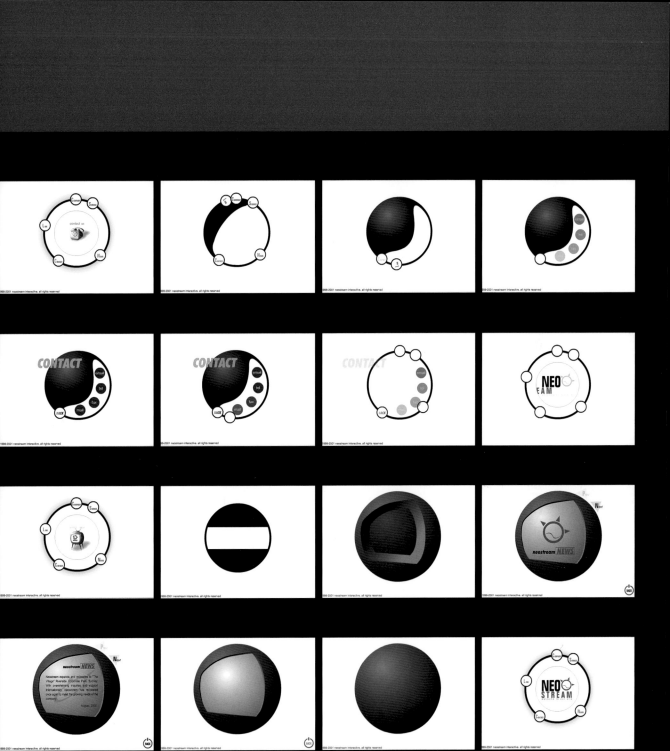

Ford Motor Company

 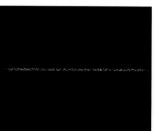  

自動車製造・販売／Automobile Manufacture & Sales　　GERMANY

フォード・モーター・カンパニーのフラッシュサイト。ストップウオッチのようなコントローラーが印象的。フォード社のデザインとテクノロジー、イノベイションについて、内容の濃いコンテンツが充実している。スピード感、高級感のあるサイトだ。

Ford Motor Company's Flash site. The stopwatch-type controller is impressive. Rich content includes Ford designs, technologies and innovations; the site gives the feeling of both speed and high quality.

| Soft ware : A, B-2, B-3, E-2 | CL : Ogilvy & Mather, Detroit | DF : EYE4U active media, Munich |

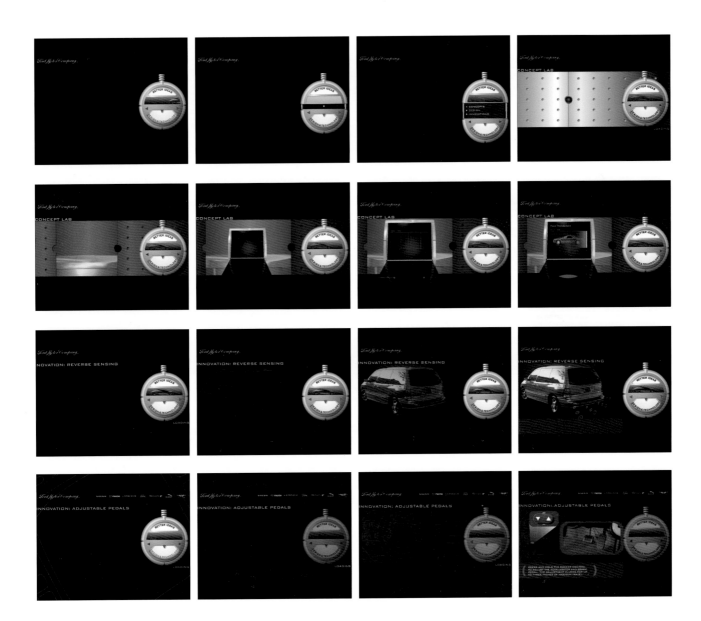

Ford Motor Company
SAFETY FEATURES

BETTER IDEAS
DESIGN & TECHNOLOGY

LOADING

Ford Motor Company
SAFETY FEATURES

BETTER IDEAS
DESIGN & TECHNOLOGY

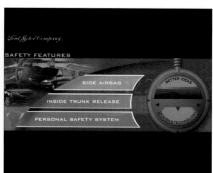

Ford Motor Company
SAFETY FEATURES

SIDE AIRBAG
INSIDE TRUNK RELEASE
PERSONAL SAFETY SYSTEM

BETTER IDEAS
DESIGN & TECHNOLOGY

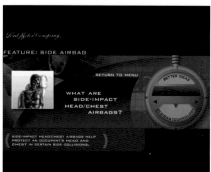

Ford Motor Company
FEATURE: SIDE AIRBAG

RETURN TO MENU

WHAT ARE
SIDE-IMPACT
HEAD/CHEST
AIRBAGS?

BETTER IDEAS
DESIGN & TECHNOLOGY

SIDE-IMPACT HEAD/CHEST AIRBAGS HELP
PROTECT AN OCCUPANT'S HEAD AND
CHEST IN CERTAIN SIDE COLLISIONS.

Ford Motor Company
FEATURE: INSIDE TRUNK RELEASE

RETURN TO MENU

THIS SUMMER,
FORD MOTOR COMPANY WILL
BECOME THE FIRST AUTOMAKER
TO MAKE A STANDARD EMERGENCY
TRUNK RELEASE SYSTEM ON A RANGE OF

BETTER IDEAS
DESIGN & TECHNOLOGY

THE INSIDE TRUNK RELEASE IS A
STANDARD OPTION ON THE TAURUS
AND SABLE 2000 AND WILL BE
PHASED INTO OTHER MODELS.

Ford Motor Company
FEATURE: PERSONAL SAFETY SYSTEM

BETTER IDEAS
DESIGN & TECHNOLOGY

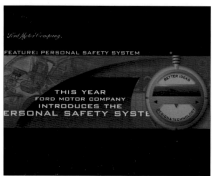

Ford Motor Company
FEATURE: PERSONAL SAFETY SYSTEM

THIS YEAR
FORD MOTOR COMPANY
INTRODUCES THE
PERSONAL SAFETY SYSTE

BETTER IDEAS
DESIGN & TECHNOLOGY

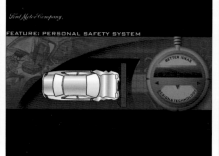

Ford Motor Company
FEATURE: PERSONAL SAFETY SYSTEM

BETTER IDEAS
DESIGN & TECHNOLOGY

Ford Motor Company
FEATURE: PERSONAL SAFETY SYSTEM

RETURN TO MENU

AN ELECTRONIC SENSOR
SYSTEM ESTIMATES THE
SEVERITY OF THE CRASH,
AND PROVIDES THAT
INFORMATION TO OTHER
SYSTEM COMPONENTS.

BETTER IDEAS
DESIGN & TECHNOLOGY

NEW REMOTE-MOUNTED CRASH
SEVERITY SENSOR

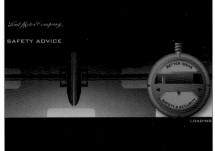
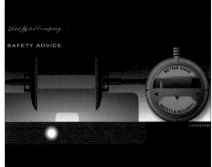

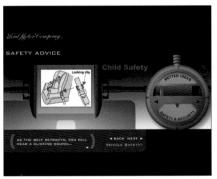
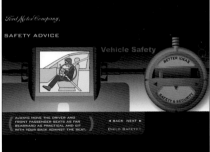
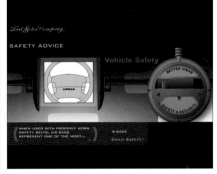

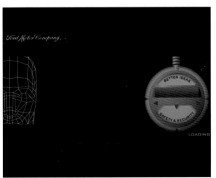

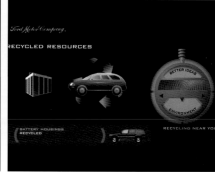

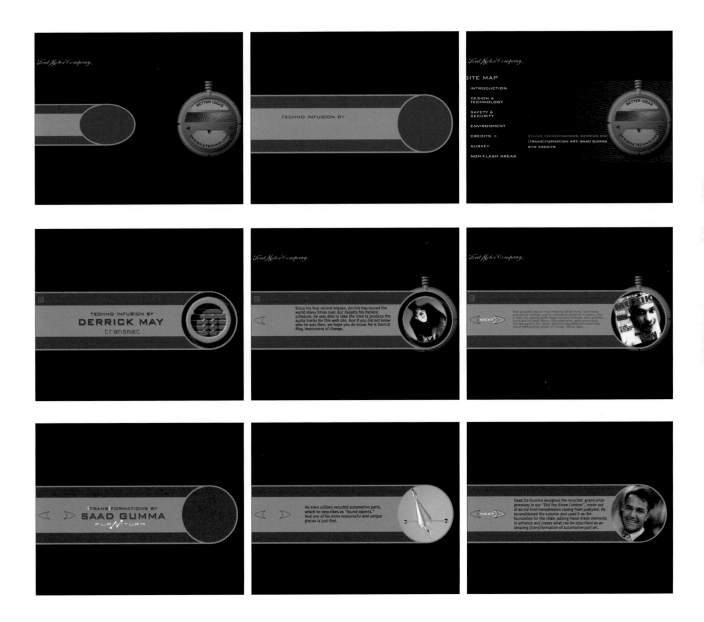

Peter Hielscher

http://www.hielscher.de

  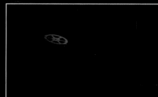 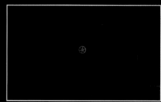

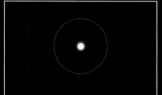   

映画＆TV制作／Film & TV Production　　**GERMANY**

ミュンヘンのフィルム＆ビデオプロダクション「Peter Hielscher」のサイト。3Dグラフィックスで描かれた精密でレトロなデザインのアイテムが、ゲームのように動いて気持ちいい。ちょっと近未来的なイメージを感じさせる。サイトプロデュースはEYE4U。

Peter Hielscher is a film and video production company in Munich. Detailed 3D graphic design items with a retro look move around smoothly, as if in a game. The site also contains some images of the future. Produced by EYE4U.

Soft ware : A, B-2, B-3, E-2　　CL : Peter Hielscher Videoproduktion GmbH　　DF : EYE4U active media, Munich

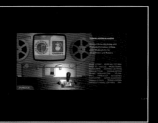

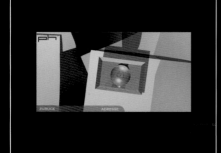

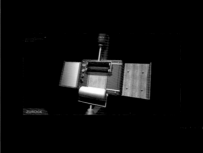

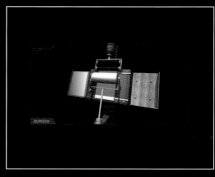

IMPRESS SOFTWARE

http://www.eye4u.com/showroom/impress/index.html

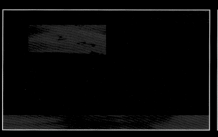

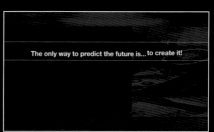

Why do business any other way?

IMPRESS® SOFTWARE

GERMANY / ソフトウェア開発／Software Development

欧米を中心に国際的な展開を続けているソフトウエア・カンパニー、IMPRESS SOFTWARE。自社のサイト内にも設置されているイメージムービーで、アッパーなテクノミュージックをバックにビデオクリップ調に仕上げている。2分以上もあって見ごたえあり。

Software company, IMPRESS SOFTWARE, develops internationally around Europe and America. The image movie installed in the site of own company using the up-tempo techno music looks like a video clip. It has more than two minutes and are very impressive.

Soft ware : A, B-2, B-3　　　CL : Impress Software AG, Hannover/Germany　　　DF : EYE4U active media, Munich

UNIMARK AG

http://www.unimark.ch/index_flash.html

マーケティング・販促／Marketing & Sales Promotion　**GERMANY**

スイスの会社「UNIMARK」のサイト。サイトプロデュースはドイツのEYE4U。

The Web site of Unimark, a Swiss company. Produced by Eye4U in Germany.popular among customers.

Soft ware : A, B-2, B-3　　CL : Unimark AG, Switzerland　　DF : EYE4U active media, Munich

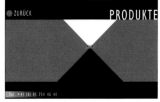
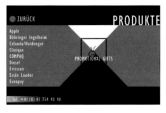

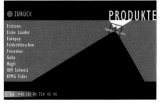

EYE4U ACTIVE MEDIA

http://www.eye4u.com

   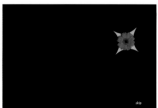

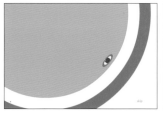  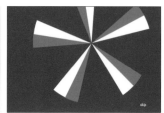 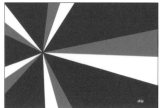

 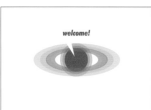 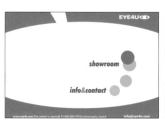 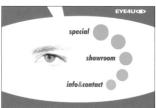

マルチメディア制作／Multimedia Production　　**GERMANY**

優れたサイトを多く手掛けているeye4uの自社サイト。ポップな色使いとダイナミックな動きはさすがの一言。ローディングからオープニング、そして各項目への流れが途切れることがない。

The Web site of Eye4U, a design company responsible for the creation of many outstanding Web projects. The use of pop colors and dynamic movement is marvelous. From the loading sequence to the opening screen, and to each contents section within, the smoothness of flow is never interrupted by the change of pages.

Soft ware : A, B-2, B-3　　CL : EYE4U active media, Munich　　DF : EYE4U active media, Munich

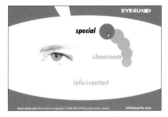

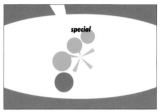

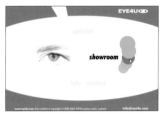

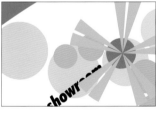

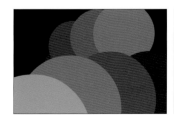
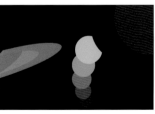

027

MANAGEMENT+ARTISTS

http://www.managementartists.com/index_flash.html

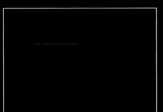

フォトグラファーエージェンシー／Photographers Agents　　**FRANCE**

美術、現代美術、写真などのアーティストをフォローする「MANAGEMENT+ARTISTS」のオフィシャル・サイト。オープニングのクールでグラフィカルなムービーと、スピーチマネージャーによるテキストリーディングがあり、サイトのコンセプトを端的に表している。

MANAGEMENT+ARTISTS's official site. The company promotes artists in the art, modern art and photography disciplines. The cool, graphical opening movie and text reading by the speech manager best represent the site's concept.

| Soft ware : A, B-1, B-2 | CL : MANAGEMENT ARTISTS | DF : Bronx interactive |

SPORTIFS ON LINE (1)

http://www.isabelleblanc.com/

FRANCE スポーツ用品オンライン通販／Online Sports Portal

シンプルな温度計のローディングムービー。スノーボードの各アイテムがフラッシュで流れるオープニングは、センスのよさを表している。競技種目のスラローム等のスノーボードを専門とするサイト。選手のインタビューや各大会の結果等が掲載されている。

A simple thermometer is shown during the loading sequence. Various snowboarding items appear in the Flash opening, which has a good design sense. The site specializes in competitive snowboarding events such as the slalom, and includes athlete interviews and competition reports.

Soft ware : A, B-1, B-2　　　CL : SPORTIFSONLINE　　　DF : Bronx interactive

SPORTIFS ON LINE (2)

http://www.ericpoujade.com/

スポーツ用品オンライン通販／Online Sports Portal　FRANCE

Eric Poujadeのオフィシャルサイト。オープニングに現われる、ワイヤーフレームとシルエットで描かれた鞍馬（体操競技の）の動きは秀逸。コンテンツも充実しており、インタビューやヒストリーなど読みごたえあり。サイトに興味がなくてもムービーは必見だ。

Eric Poujade's official site. The wire frame renderings and the movement of the pommel horse in silhouette at the opening are outstanding. Rich content, interviews and histories make for interesting reading. The site includes a movie that is worth watching, even if you are not interested in the site.

Soft ware : A, B-1, B-2, F　　CL : SPORTIFSONLINE　　DF : Bronx interactive

MARITHÉ+FRANÇOIS GIRBAUD (1)

http://www.girbaud.com/eng/home.html

FRANCE ファッションデザイナー／**Fashion Designer**

ヨーロピアン・ジーンズで長い歴史を持つマリテ＋フランソワ・ジルボーのサイト。コレクション同様、サイトもアヴァンギャルドでクリエイティビティ。映画のオープニングようにスタートしながら流れるようにコンテンツが進む。日本語のサイトにも注目。http://www.takaya.co.jp/girbaud/

The Web site of Marithé François Girbaud, a European jeans maker with a long history. As is their collection, the Web site is avant-garde and creative. The movie-like opening flows smoothly into contents. There is also a Japanese language site.

Soft ware : A, B-1, B-2, F　　　CL : Marithé+François Girbaud　　　DF : Bronx interactive

MARITHÉ+FRANçOIS GIRBAUD (2)

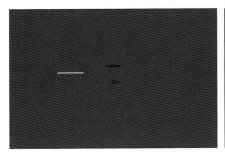

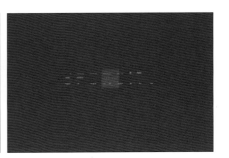

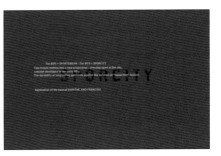

MARITHÉ+FRANÇOIS GIRBAUD (4)

http://www.girbaud.com/eng/pages/denim/denim_index.html

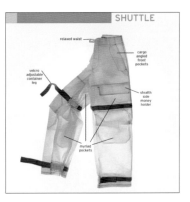

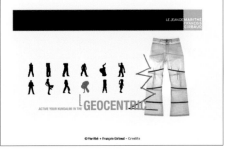

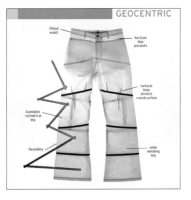

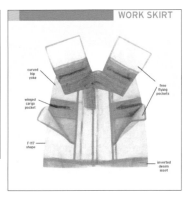

MARITHÉ+FRANçOIS GIRBAUD (5)

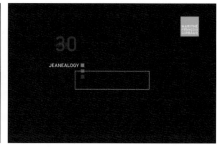

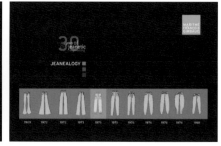

MARITHÉ+FRANÇOIS GIRBAUD (6)

http://www.girbaud.com/eng/pages/jeaneatic/morpho_index.html

  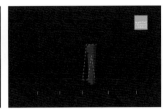 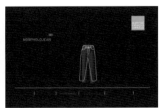

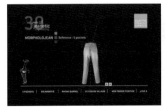   
 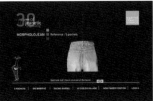 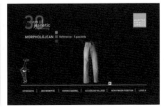 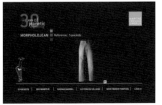

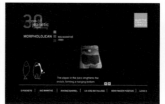

MARITHÉ+FRANÇOIS GIRBAUD (7)

http://www.girbaud.com/eng/pages/footwear/footwear_index.html   http://www.girbaud.com/eng/pages/defile/defile_index.html

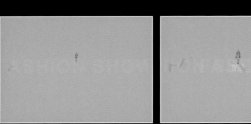

MARITHÉ+FRANçOIS GIRBAUD (8)

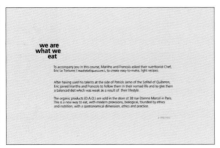

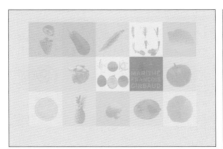

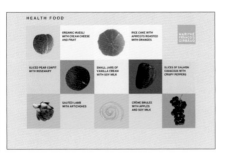

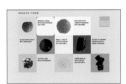

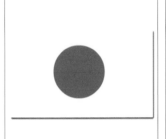

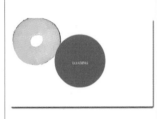

ORGANIC MUESLI WITH CREAM CHEESE AND FRUIT : MUESLI

Ingrédients: (4 people)

cream cheese: 400gr
muesli 80g
strawberries: 50g
apples: 50 g
blueberries: 70g
raspberries: 70g
liquid organic sugar

Cut the apple and the strawberries in small pieces,
add the cream cheese,blueberries and raspberries
add 3 spoonfuls of liquid sugar, and mix the ingredients very well
with a wooden spoon.
Pour the cream cheese with the fruit in a shallow plate.
At the last moment, sprinkle with muesli.

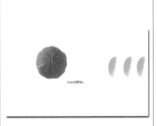

RICE CAKE WITH APRICOTS ROASTED WITH ORANGES

Ingrédients: (4 people)

thai white rice: 100 g
sugar: 50 gr+80 g
milk: 600ml
vanilla Pod: 1/2
eggs: 2
raisins: 50 g
apricots: 6
butter: 20 g
orange juice: 1
liquid organic sugar

Wash the rice with cold water, pour the rice in the milk add 50g of sugar,
cut the vanilla in two and scrape out the small black seeds. Cover, and let
cook over low heat for 30 minutes, stirring from time to time. With 40g of
sugar, create a caramel, pour it into small ramekins, and let it cool down.
Beat the eggs, add the rice little by little, mix with a wooden spatula, add
the raisins, pour this mixture into the ramekins, cook it in a double
saucepan in the oven for 25 minutes at 170 degrees, then let it cool. Cut
the apricots in fours, in a hot frying pan melt the butter, add the
apricots, moisten two soup spoons with liquid sugar, cook 1 minute, deglaze
with the orange juice, cook 2 minutes. In the middle of a plate, put the

CRÈME BRULEE WITH APPLES AND SOY MILK

Ingrédients: (4 people)

egg yolk: 5
whole egg:1
vanilla Pod:1
sugar: 70g
soy milk: 500ml
golden Apple: 250g

Peel the apple, cut in small pieces, back 10 minutes in a casserole pan with
half of the juice of a lemon and a little water, and crush with a fork to
create marmalade, let it cool. Boil the soymilk with the vanilla split in
two lengthwise, let it infuse for 10 minutes. Whiten the egg yolks and whole
eggs with sugar add the milk little by little, strain it. Place in flat
ramekins, cover lightly with the apple marmalade, pour the crème, bake in a
double saucepan for 45 minutes at 110 then let it cool. Sprinkle the crème
with moist brown sugar, caramelize it under the broiler.

MARITHÉ+FRANÇOIS GIRBAUD (9)

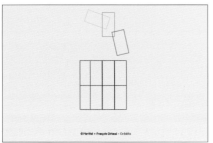

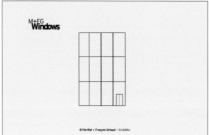

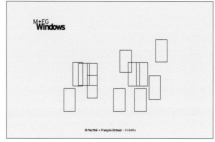

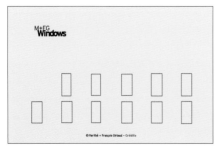

MARITHÉ+FRANÇOIS GIRBAUD (10)

http://www.girbaud.com/eng/pages/presse/presse_index.html http://www.girbaud.com/eng/pages/boutik/boutique_index.html

MARITHÉ+FRANÇOIS GIRBAUD (11)

http://www.girbaud.com/eng/pages/pdv/pdv_index.html

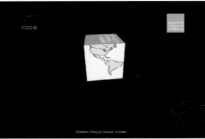

MARITHÉ+FRANÇOIS GIRBAUD (12)

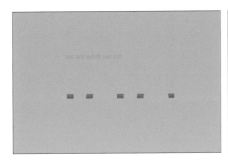

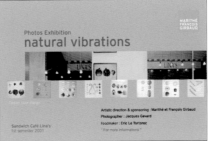

Bronx

http://www.bronxinteractive.com

ウェブデザイン／Website Agency　　FRANCE

多くの優れたウェブをデザインしている「Bronx」のサイト。愛嬌のあるキャラクターが登場。ロボットのようなキャラクターの動きがいい。ボタンをクリックすると、まるで新しいカードがファイリングされていくように上に上に重なっていく。左上の○を軸に少しづつズレていくのがおもしろい。

Site of "Bronx" designing a lot of superior Web. A cute character appears. Robot-like movement of a character is good. When a user clicks a button, it is piled up as if the new cards were filing. It is interesting to slip off centering on ○ on the left.

Soft ware : A, B-1, B-2, F　　　CL : Bronx interactive　　　DF : Bronx interactive

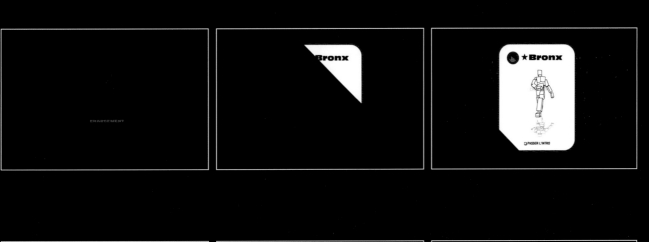

Bembo's ZOO
http://www.bemboszoo.com

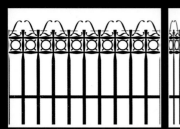

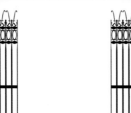

Bembo'

Bembo's
ZOO

Bembo's
ZOO

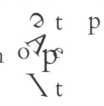

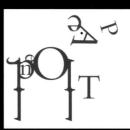

A B C D E F G
H I J K L M
N O P Q R S T
U V W X Y Z

Antelope

出版社／Publishing House　　USA

出版社「Henry Holt」のサイト。サイト名が "Bembo's ZOO" だけあって、画面上の好きなアルファベットを選んでクリックすると、その文字を頭文字とした名前の動物が、その文字によって形成されるというおもしろい趣向のモーショングラフィックス。

Site of publishing company "Henry Holt." As the site name fits "Bembo's ZOO," a user selects and clicks the favorite alphabet on a screen the alphabet forms shape of animal which name has same initial. It is interesting motion graphics to create the animals with letters.

Soft ware : A, B-1, B-3, P　　　　CL : Henry Holt　　　　DF : Mucca Design

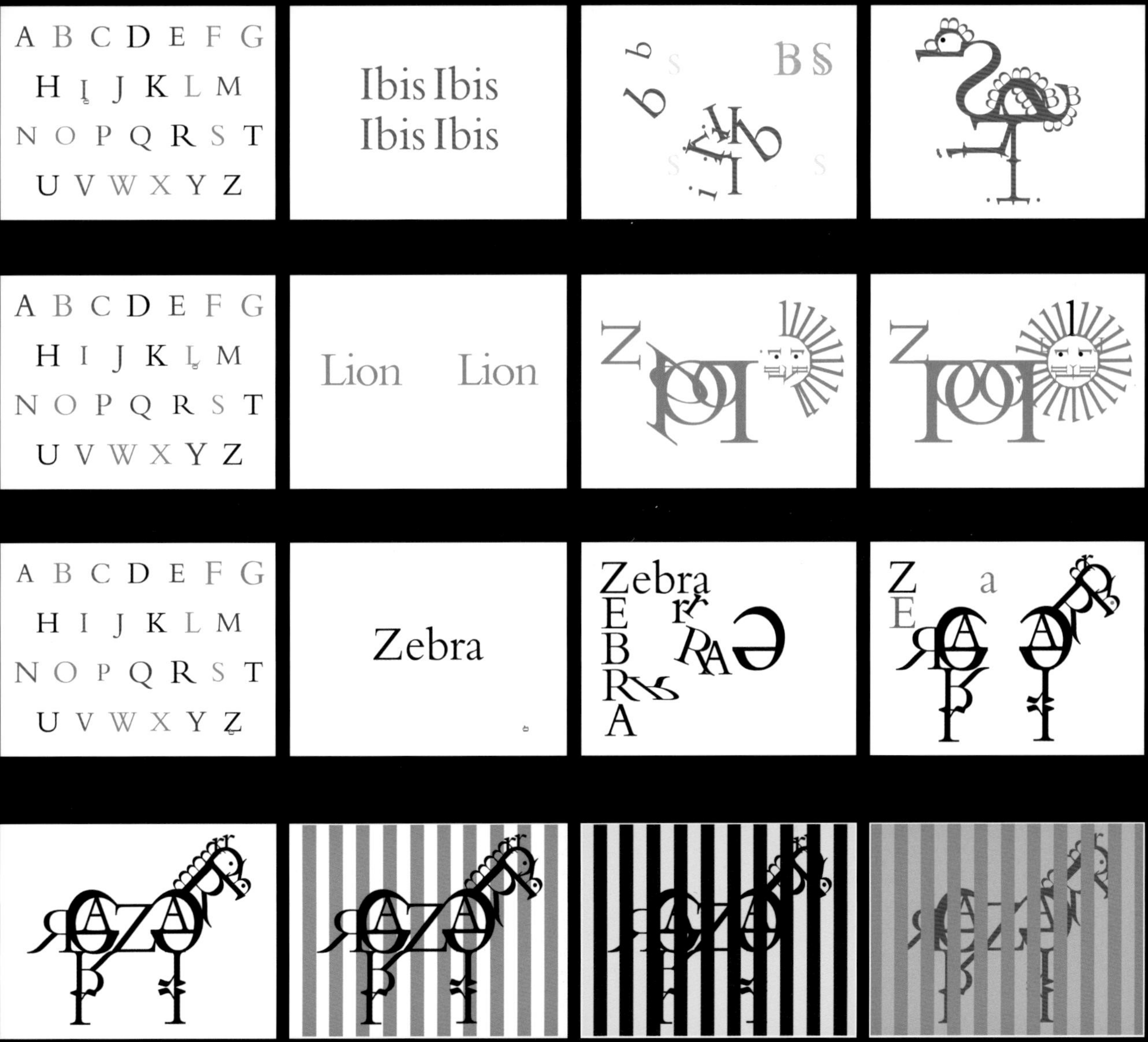
A B C D E F G
H I J K L M
N O P Q R S T
U V W X Y Z
Ibis Ibis
Ibis Ibis
A B C D E F G
H I J K L M
N O P Q R S T
U V W X Y Z
Lion Lion
A B C D E F G
H I J K L M
N O P Q R S T
U V W X Y Z
Zebra
Zebra

Avantgarde
http://www.avantgarde.de/av_flash.html

  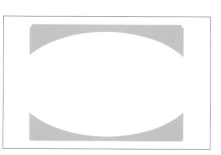

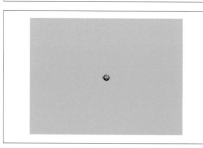 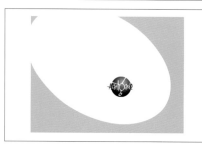 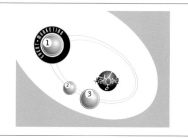

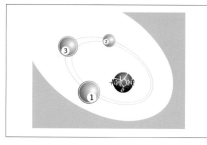  

イベント制作／Event Agency　**GERMANY**

マーケティングやプロモーションを行うドイツのカンパニー、Avantgarde。印象的なロゴマークと同様、ビリヤードのボールをモチーフにして各コンテンツがサクサクと動く。テキストがメインなので派手な動きこそないが、カンパニーコンセプトがよく伝わるサイトだ。

The Web site of Avantgarde, a German company that specializes in marketing and promotion. Each content element moves quickly in a billiard ball design motif that also incorporates the company's impressive logo mark. Although the movement is not showy , the site successfully communicates company concepts.

| Soft ware : A, B-1 | CL : Avantgarde | DF : coma2 - collective of media artists |

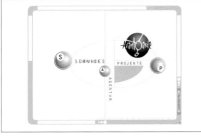
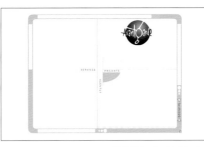

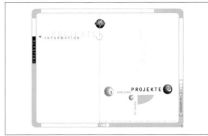

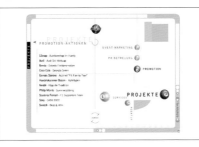
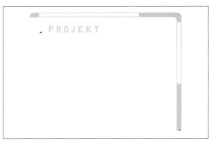

COMPAQ

http://www.coma2.de/ipaq/

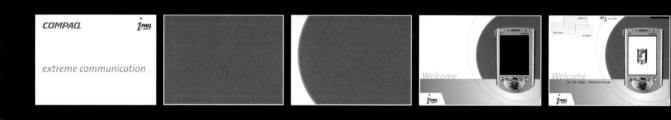

コンピューター製造・販売／Computer Manufacture & Sales　　GERMANY

コンパック社のPDA、iPAQのサイト。ローディングムービーをオープニングとし、シンプルでわかりやすいインターフェースへと続く。大きなコンテンツはハードウエア、ソフトウエア、アクセサリ。テキストは少なく、ビジュアルで商品イメージを定着させている。

The Web site of iPAQ, Compaq's PDA. Beginning with a movie while loading, the site continues to a simple and user-friendly interface. Major contents are categorized as hardware, software, and accessories. The product image is enforced by visuals, with a minimum use of text.

Soft ware : A, B-1, B-2　　　CL : COMPAQ Computer　　　DF : coma2 - collective of media artists

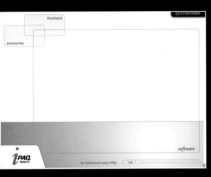

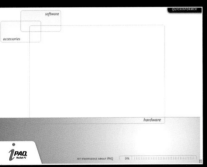

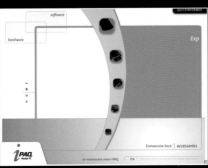
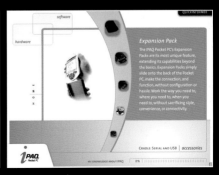

CAZAL-EYEWEAR
http://www.cazal-eyewear.com

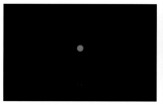 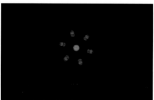 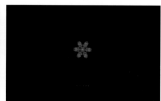 

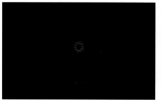   

アイウェアデザイン／Eyewear Design Company　**GERMANY**

アイウエアブランド、CAZALのオフィシャルサイト。スローな動きとアンビエントなBGMでサイトのオリジナリティを出している。インターフェースのデザインはアイウエアのブランドだけにもちろん眼。わかりやすく見やすいサイトだ。

The official Web site of CAZAL, an eyewear brand. The slow motion and ambient music express the site's originality. Needless to say, the interface design uses an eye as its motif. It is simple, and easy to navigate.

Soft ware : A, B-1　　　CL : CAZAL-EYEWEAR　　　DF : coma2 - collective of media artists

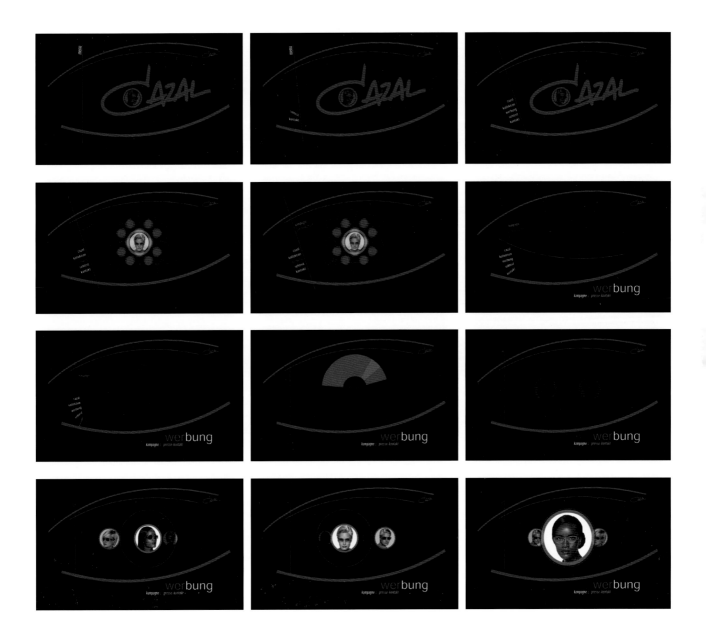

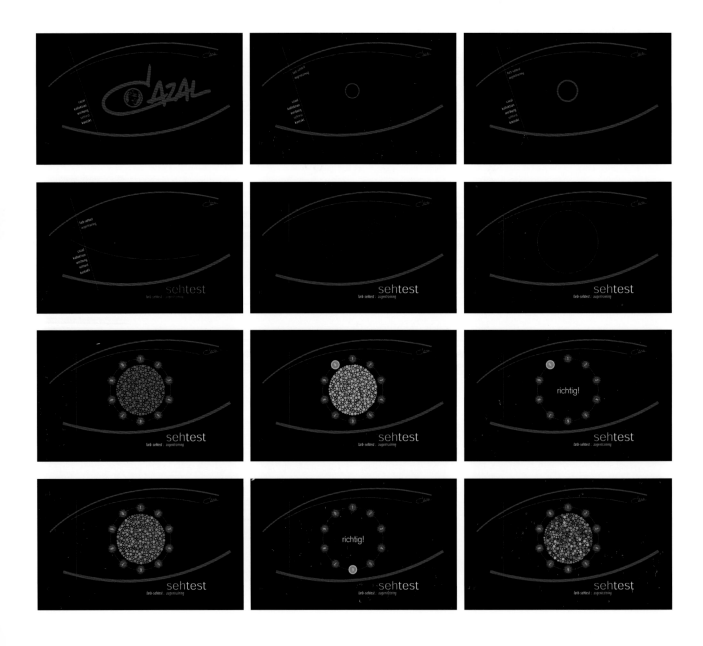

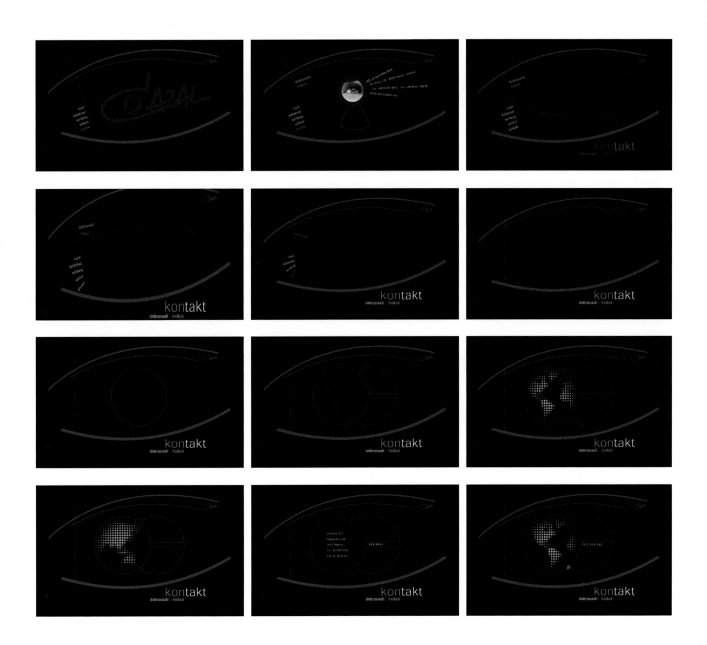

MTV

http://www.mtv2.co.uk/html/index2.html

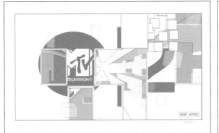  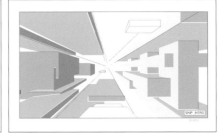

  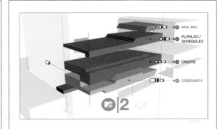

音楽TVチャンネル／Music Television Channel　**UK**

音楽専門チャンネル「MTV」のサイト。ジングルやQカットでアイデンティティを主張してきた局だけにウエブも充実した内容。スケジュールやコミュニティもあるので、ポータルにする人も多いはずだが、その際に、飽きさせないデザインというものは難しい。

This is the UK Web site of music channel MTV2. Contents are rich and varied, with the channel's jingles and Q cuts emphasizing its identity. While most portals are not designed a way that will continue to hold interest, it is likely that many people will use this portal to access program schedules and communities.

Soft ware : A　　CL : MTV　　DF : Digit Digital Experiences Ltd

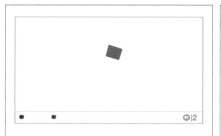

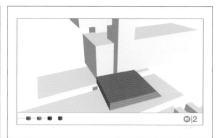
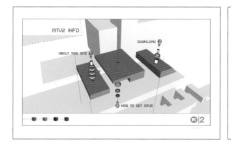
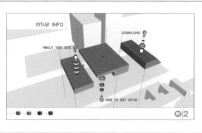
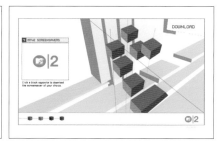
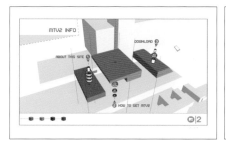
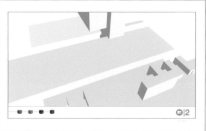
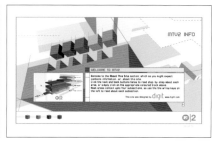

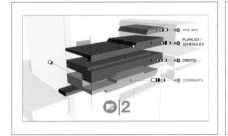

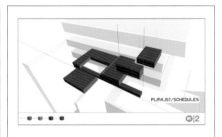

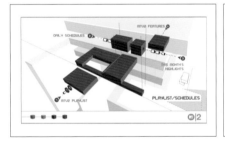

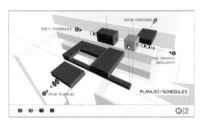

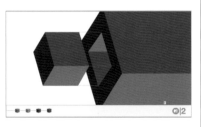

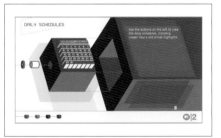

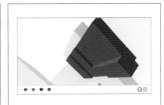

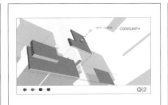
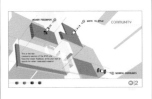
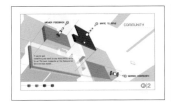

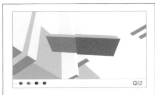
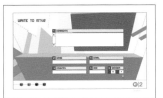

HOOVER

2002年3月現在、インターネット上で見ることができません。　As of March 2002, this Website was no longer available.

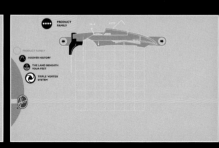
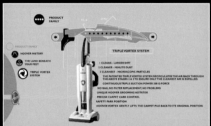
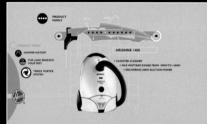
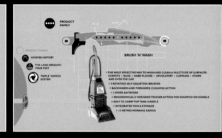
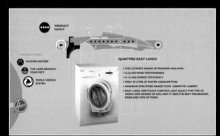
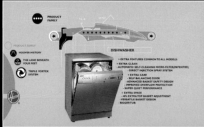
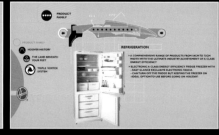

電化製品製造／Electrical Products Manufacturer　　**UK**

イギリスの老舗家電メーカー、HOOVER。イギリスでは掃除機のことを一般的にHOOVERと呼ぶそうだ。それほどポピュラーなメーカーのサイトにもかかわらず、構造はシンプルで見やすい。サイトのコンセプトがしっかりしていないと、アレもコレもになってしまうものだ。

The Web site of Hoover, a traditional electric appliance manufacturer located in England. Although it is the Web site of a major corporation (vacuum cleaners are called "Hoovers" in England), it has a simple and easy-to-understand structure. This has been realized by having a clear production concept.

Soft ware : A, B-1, B-2　　　CL : HOOVER　　　DF : Deepend, London

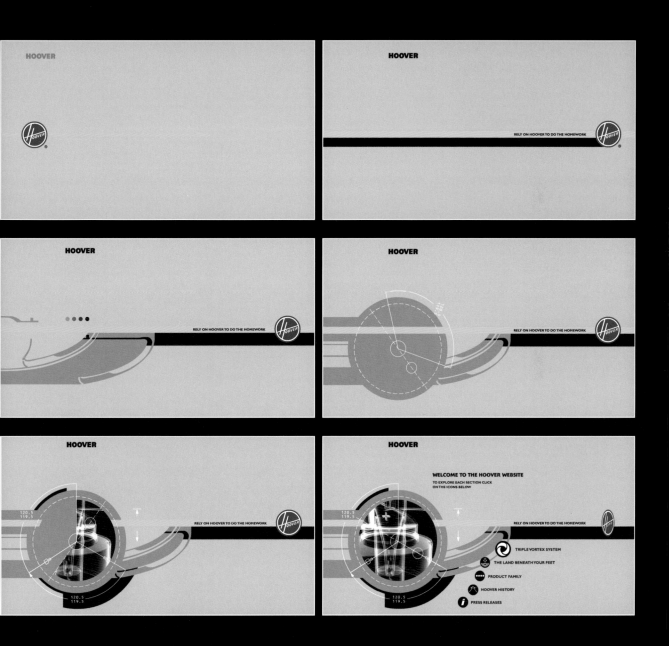

>> **HOOVER**

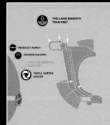
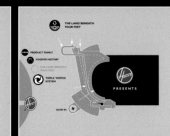

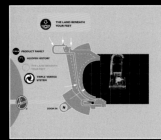
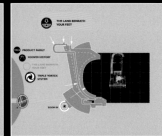
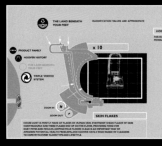

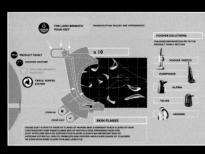

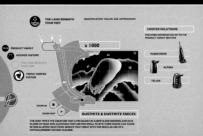

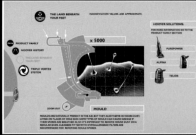

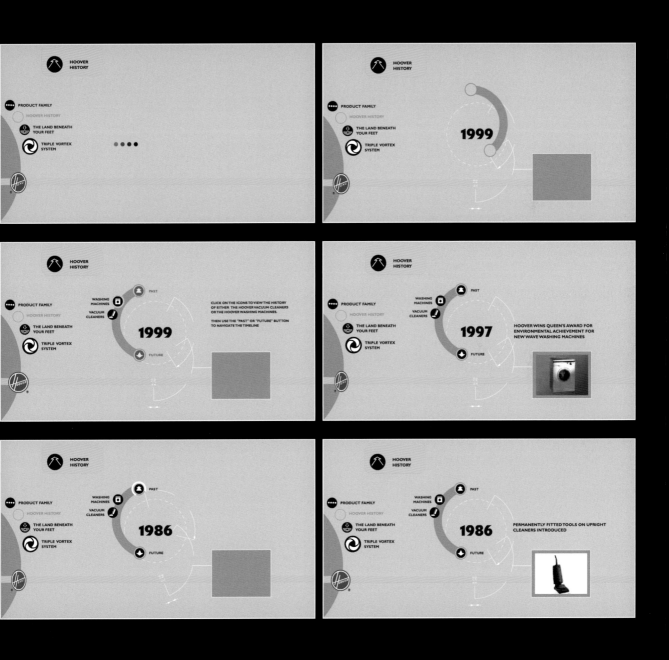

>> HOOVER

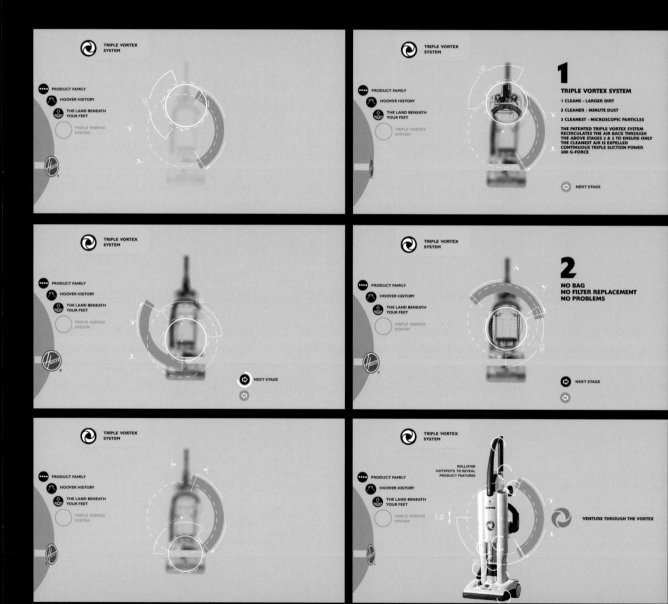

TRIPLE VORTEX SYSTEM

PRODUCT FAMILY
HOOVER HISTORY
THE LAND BENEATH YOUR FEET
TRIPLE VORTEX SYSTEM

1

TRIPLE VORTEX SYSTEM

1 CLEANS - LARGER DIRT

2 CLEANER - MINUTE DUST

3 CLEANEST - MICROSCOPIC PARTICLES

THE PATENTED TRIPLE VORTEX SYSTEM RECIRCULATES THE AIR BACK THROUGH THE ABOVE STAGES 2 & 3 TO ENSURE ONLY THE CLEANEST AIR IS EXPELLED CONTINUOUS TRIPLE SUCTION POWER 300 G-FORCE

NEXT STAGE

NEXT STAGE

2

NO BAG
NO FILTER REPLACEMENT
NO PROBLEMS

NEXT STAGE

ROLLOVER HOTSPOTS TO REVEAL PRODUCT FEATURES

VENTURE THROUGH THE VORTEX

CARTOON NETWORK

http://www.cartoonnetwork.co.uk/microsites/toonami/html/index.html

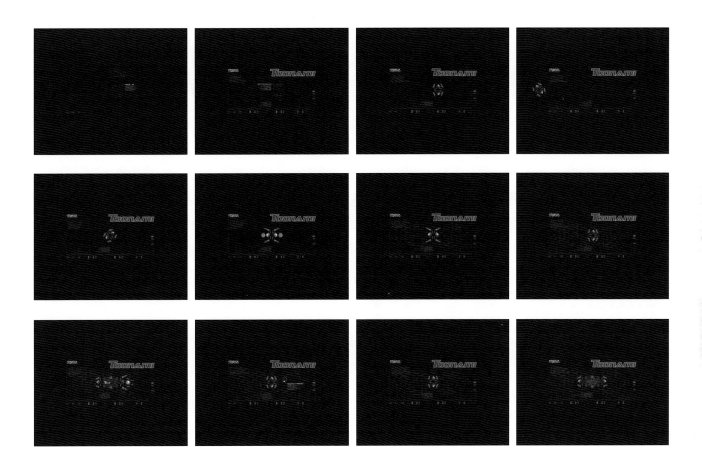

UK　エンターテインメント配信／Broadcast & Entertainment Network

アニメ専門のテレビ局、カートゥーンネットワークのサイト。バットマン、バグスバニーからトムとジェリーまで、懐かしいアメコミのキャラに出会えるほか、ネットワーク上でフラッシュゲームを楽しむことができる。オンラインで本編を視聴することも可能。

Web site of The Cartoon Network, a TV channel that specializes in animation. On the site, you will encounter such nostalgic American comic characters as Batman, Bugs Bunny, and Tom and Jerry. You can play Flash games and watch programs on-line.

Soft ware : A, B-1　　CL : CARTOON NETWORK / TOONAMI　　DF : Deepend, London

NEW ORDER GET READY

http://www.newordergetready.com

 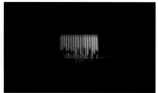  

 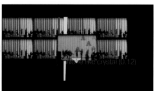  

 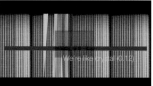  

レコードレーベル／**Record Label**　　**UK**

レコードレーベル「WEA London Records」のサイト。鮮やかな色使いと、音楽を感じさせるグラフィックスが、流れるように展開していく美しいサイト。インタラクティブな要素も含まれ、カーソルをたどってラインアートが表現されていく。

Site of record label "WEA London Records." The beautiful site using vivid color and graphics, giving the sense of music, develops smoothly. An interactive element is included, and line art will be expressed by following a cursor.

Soft ware : A, B-2

CL : WEA London Records

DF : Deepend, London

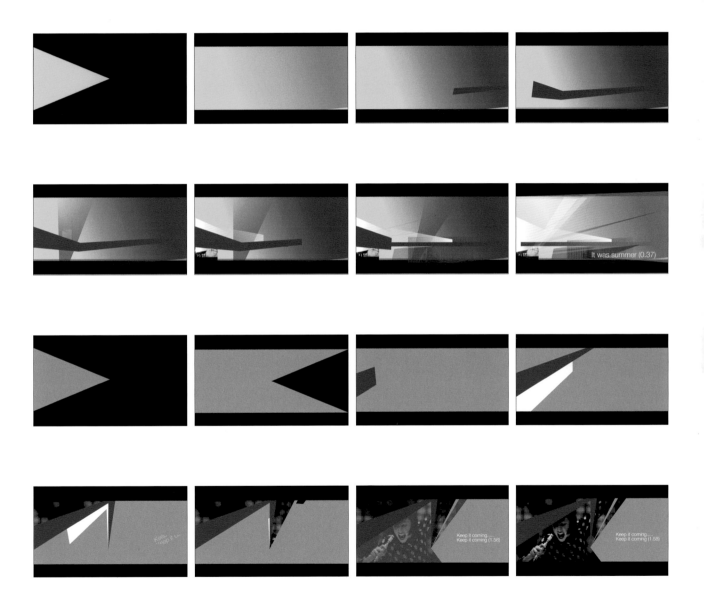

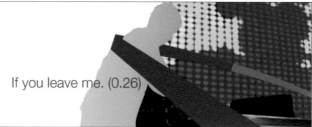

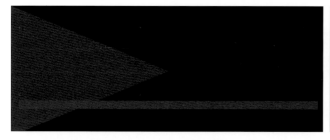

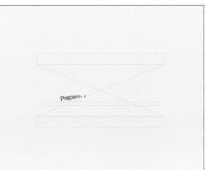

軍艦島 Gunkanjima

http://www.ambixious.co.jp/g3/flash.htm

 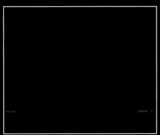  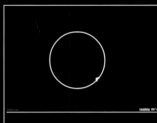

   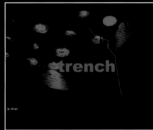

ウェブサイト＆グラフィックデザイン／Website & Graphic Design　　JAPAN

フィルムのノイズ風なローディングでスタートする「軍艦島」はその名の通り、長崎の軍艦島を紹介しているサイト。大正時代からコンクリート製のマンションが立ち並んだ海底炭坑の島。今はもちろん無人で、廃虚と化しているが、それは耽美であったりもする。

While loading, the "Gunkanjima" screen is filled with visual film "noise." As the name indicates, this site introduces Gunkanjima Island in Nagasaki, where coal had been mined underwater since the Taisho era. Although the island's rows of concrete apartment buildings are now in ruins and uninhabited, the island is somehow esthetically beautiful.

| Soft ware : A | CL：細川タロヲ／Taro Hosokawa | DF：細川タロヲ／Taro Hosokawa |

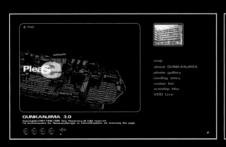

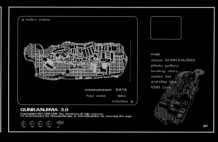

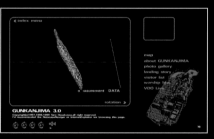

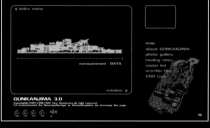

>> 軍艦島 GunkanJima

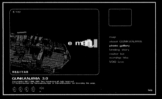

AIGA

http://www.thunkdesign.com/v3/clients/aigarr/rr01.html

グラフィックデザイン協会／Non-profit Graphic Design Community   USA

デザイン事務所「THUNKdesign」のサイト内で紹介されているアメリカのグラフィックデザイン協会「American Institute of Graphic Arts (AIGA)」のサイト。赤、黄、黒を組み合わせた警戒色に、サイレンをイメージしたサウンドが注意を引く。軽快なモーショングラフィックスが小気味良い。

A site by the design house THUNKdesign. Created to introduce a conference organized by the American Institute of Graphic Arts (AIGA), a graphic design association. An arresting, siren-like sound works well with the red, yellow, and black color motif. The light motion graphics are also smart.

Soft ware : A, B-1, B-2, B-4, C, G-2, K	CL : American Institute of Graphic Arts (AIGA)	DF : THUNKdesign

rom

TWIX

http://www.thunkdesign.com/v3/clients/twix/twix03.html

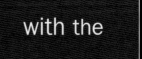

USA 菓子製造／Snack Food Company

デザイン事務所「THUNKdesign」のサイト内で紹介されているアメリカの菓子メーカー「Twix」のサイト。チョコレート、キャラメルが練り合わさっていくような イメージのイントロアニメが展開。コンテンツボタンにカーソルを合わせると、スナックをかじった時のような音が出て効果的。

The design house THUNKdesign introduces a site it created for the American confectioner Twix. The intro cartoon features a chocolate with a parade of caramel on top, slowly developing on screen. Visitors hear a satisfying chomping sound when they pass the cursor over the contents buttons.

Soft ware : A, B-1, B-2, D-3, G-2, K   CL : TWIX / M&M Mars   DF : THUNKdesign

EDDIE BAUER

http://www.thunkdesign.com/v3/clients/eb/eb05.html

  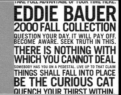 

カジュアルウェア製造・販売／Casual Clothing Retailer　　**USA**

デザイン事務所「THUNKdesign」のサイト内で紹介されているカジュアルウェアメーカー「Eddie Bauer」のサイト。とある一日の生活を、それぞれ違う人の視点から展開しているムービーが臨場感溢れ、そこに登場する人物がEddie Bauerのウェア等を身につけていて、効果的な広告となっている。

The design house THUNKdesign introduces the site it created for the apparel retailer Eddie Bauer. The shifting viewpoints of the models featured on the page enhance the sense of "realness." The site effectively introduces and advertises Eddie Bauer's apparel.

Soft ware : A, B-1, B-2, D-3, G-2, K, L　　CL : Eddie Bauer　　DF : THUNKdesign

no.046

Presentation & Interactive

Lookandfeel new media
http://www.lookadfeel.com

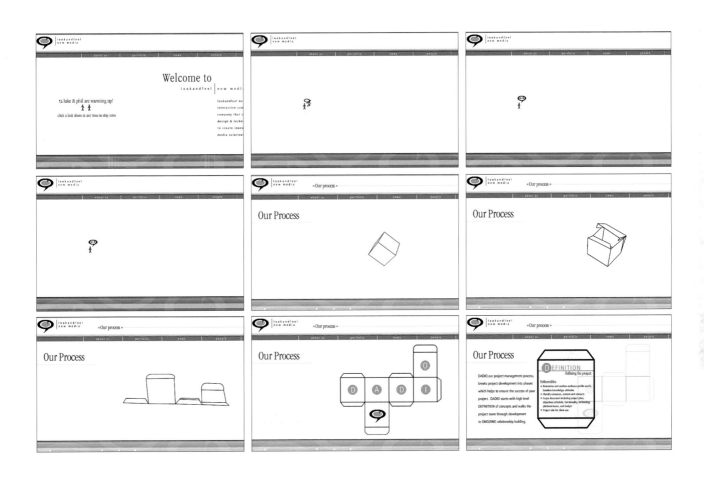

USA インタラクティブコミュニケーション／**Interactive Communications Company**

ウエブデザインからマルチメディアコンテンツ全般を手掛けるLOOK&FEEL NEW MEDIAのサイト。カンパニーについて事細かにテキストベースで掲載。派手な動きや見ごたえのあるアニメーションこそないが、インデックスも実用的でわかりやすい。

The Web site of LookandFeel New Media, a company specializing in Web design and multimedia contents. Company details are presented in a text-based design. It is an easy-to-navigate site with a simple and practical index, without flamboyant or showy animation.

Soft ware : A　　　CL : Lookandfeel new media　　　DF : Lookandfeel new media

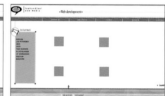

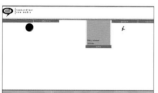

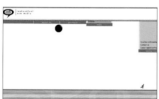

Lee DUNGAREES
http://www.leedungarees.com

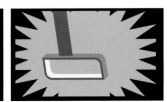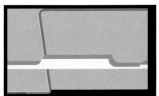
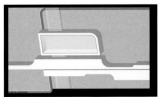

USA | **アパレル／Apparel**

ジーンズを軸としたアメリカのアパレルメーカー「Lee Jeans」のブランド「Lee Dungarees」のサイト。少しレトロな雰囲気を醸し出しているモノクロ写真とデザイン、そしてコミカルな動きが、アメリカで誕生し、今や世界的な定番ファッションとなったジーンズの歴史を思い起こさせる。

The site for Lee Dungarees, a brand of the American apparel maker, Lee Jeans. A monochrome photo and "retro" graphics bounce onto the screen with a good humorous effect. The page has a "born in America" feeling, but it actually gives a good sense of the history of jeans internationally, all the way up to the present.

Soft ware : A | CL : Lee Jeans-Lee Dungarees Brand | DF : Lookandfeel new media

>> **Lee DUNGAREES**

   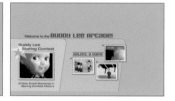

   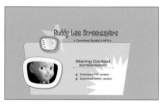

ABSOLUT

http://www.absolutdirector.com

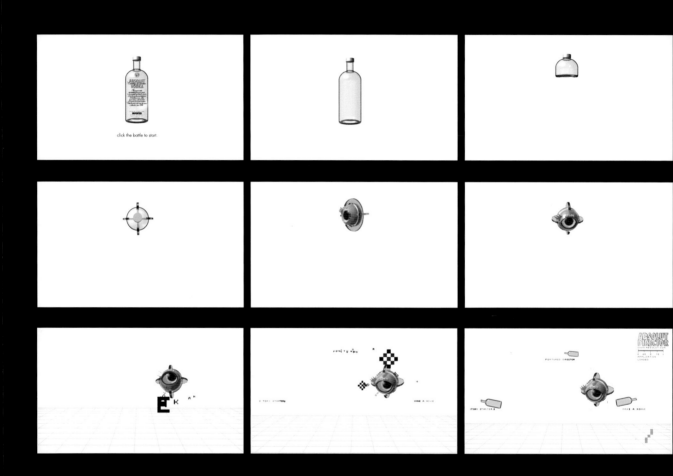

飲料製造／Beverage Manufacturer **SWEDEN**

スウェーデンの飲料メーカー「The Absolut Company」のサイト。サイト全体にわたって、趣向を凝らしたモーショングラフィックスがふんだんに使われている。ドリンクボトルから変化する目玉ロボットは機械的な声を発し、カーソルから逃げたり、目線を合わせてきたりして、怪しい雰囲気。

Site for the Swedish vodka distiller, The Absolut Company. The whole site uses dynamic graphics and an elaborate story line. Click the bottle and it transforms into Hilde, an eye-ball shaped robot that greets you with a mechanical voice. Pass the cursor over Hilde and she escapes to another part of the screen. The mood is dubious and funny.

| Soft ware : A | CL : The Absolut Company | DF : TBWA/CHIAT/DAY and Submarine |

no.058

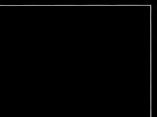 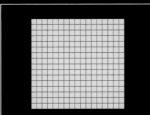 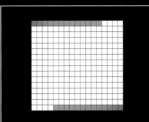 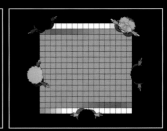

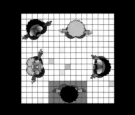 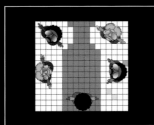 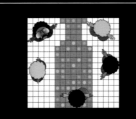 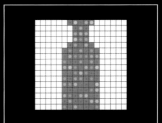

飲料製造／Beverage Manufacturer | **SWEDEN**

なつかしいディスコスタイルのキャラクターが、ディスコサウンドにのって、くるくる回る楽しいアニメーション。ダンスフロアを真上から見下ろした視点で展開される。キャラクター達の動きはフェミニンでかわいいが、顔を見ると、みなティアドロップ型のサングラスに口髭。

Fun animation of nostalgic disco-style characters dancing around with disco music. The screen is designed as if user looked down the dance floor from the top. Movement of characters is feminine and cute, but they have mustache and wear tear-drop shaped sunglasses.

Soft ware : A | CL : The Absolut Company | DF : Springtime AB

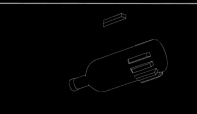

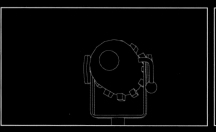

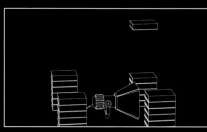

飲料製造／Beverage Manufacturer   SWEDEN

モノトーンで、テンポの良いサウンドにのって展開されるアニメーション。黒の背景に白のラインアートが栄える。視点が様々な角度に切り替わり、動きも歯切れ良い。

Monotone animation developed with tune with a quick tempo. White line art is set off against the black background. As the viewpoint is switched to various angles, the user can enjoy nimble movements.

Soft ware : A   CL : The Absolut Company   DF : TBWA/CHIAT/DAY

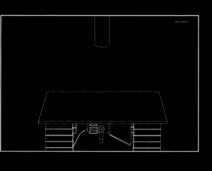 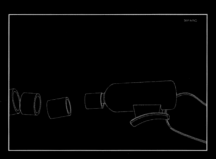 
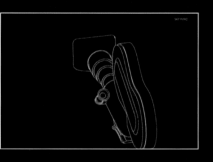 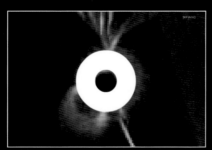 
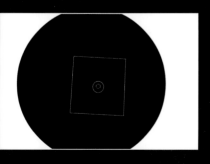 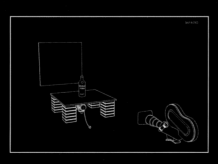 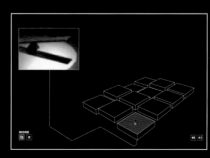

>> ABSOLUT

飲料製造／Beverage Manufacturer　　SWEDEN

レインボーカラーの細いラインの束が印象的なサイト。ABSOLUTの文字が色のラインを跨いで右から左に流れていく様は美しい。コンテンツボタンも色鮮やかで、サイト全体がセンスの良いポップアートのよう。

The site is impressed with a bunch of thin rainbow-colored lines. It is beautiful that the word "ABSOLUT" is flowed to left from right over the colorful lines. Using the bright color for the contents buttons, the whole site gives a feeling of sophisticated pop art.

| Soft ware : A | CL : The Absolut Company | DF : Springtime AB |

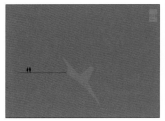   

  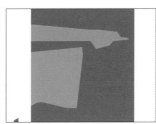 

   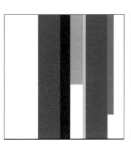 

AUSTRALIA 出版／**Publishing, Street Press**

フリーペーパーのMAP MAGAZINEのサイト。線画で描かれた飛行機のアニメーションを経て、次の各都市用のインターフェイスにジャンプ。クールなセンスでディテールまで凝っているので見ごたえバツグンだが、どこの都市にジャンプするときも同じアニメーションというのがちょっと残念。

The Site for a free paper, MAP MAGAZINE. After the animation of an airplane in line drawing, the user can jump to the interface of each city. Cool and well-detailed design makes the site worth seeing, but it is regrettable that same animation is appeared when the user jumps to any city.

Soft ware : A, B-3　　　CL : Map Magazine　　　DF : Gasket

GASKET

http://www.gasket.ws/flash.html

デザイン事務所／Design & New Media Firm　　AUSTRALIA

オーストラリアのウエブデザインの会社、GASKET。フラッシュのオープニングでは日本語で「何を表現したいのか」「他社に差をつけましょう」などの言葉がサンプリングされている。けして日本向けのサイトではないが日本語の語感をうまく利用したデザインだ。

Gasket is an Australian Web design company. The Flash opening includes Japanese sentences such as "What do you want to say?" and "Be different than your competitors." The site does not target Japanese, but does take advantage of the Japanese meanings.

Soft ware : A, B-3　　　　　CL : Map Magazine　　　　　DF : Gasket

TIM LINDGREN
http://www.gasket.ws/tim

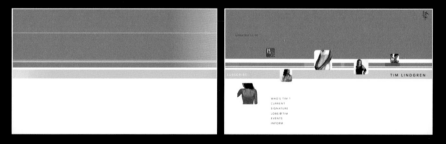

ファッション／Fashion · **AUSTRALIA**

TIM LINDGRENというオーストラリアのファッションデザイナーのサイト。モデルの写真が動き回り、見にくいというかわかりにくい。そしてBGMはなぜか中国風。ちょっと異色なスタイルが個性的といえば個性的。かすかに聞こえる波の音が叙情的だ。

The Web site of Tim Lindgren, an Australian fashion designer. Photos of models move around the screen, and it is not easy to see or understand what is happening. Chinese background music completes an unusual style and individuality. The indistinct wave sound is very lyrical.

Soft ware : A, B-3 · CL : Tim Lindgren · DF : Gasket

HOPE HARBOUR INTERNATIONAL RESORT

http://www.hopeharbourintl.com.au

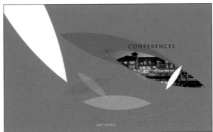

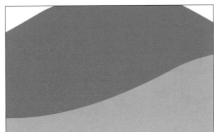
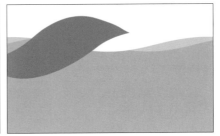

AUSTRALIA / ホテル／Hotel Resort

HOPE HARBOURというオーストラリアのリゾートホテルのサイト。高級感漂うデザインで、インフォメーションも細かく掲載されているが、なぜか BGMはアンビエントな現代音楽。リゾートテイストを感じ得ることはできない。例えばこの音楽がロビーに延々と流れていたら・・・？

The Web site of Hope Harbour, a resort hotel in Australia. The site's design is of high quality, and includes detailed information. Despite the fact that the BGM is ambient modern music, and not what you would expect to find on a resort site, the mismatch taste is interesting.

| Soft ware : A | CL : Hope Harbour International Resort | DF : Gasket |

ZOOM FILM + TV
http://www.zoomfilmtv.com.au

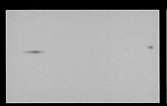   

CMプロダクション／CM Production　　**AUSTRALIA**

オーストラリアのCMプロダクション、Zoom film and televisionのサイト。ヤマハや三菱などをクライアントに持っている。サイトはCM制作が本業だけに、軽快でグルーヴがきいたスタイル。メインページのインターフェースが見づらいという難も感じるが、オリジナリティ溢れるデザインだ。

The Web site of Zoom Film and Television, a CM production company in Australia. Clients include Yamaha and Mitsubishi. The site focuses on their main business of CM production, and has a light and groovy style. The main page interface is difficult to navigate, but the overall design is full of originality.

Soft ware : A, B-3　　　　CL : Mark Toia, Zoom Film + TV　　　　DF : Gasket

lauckgroup

http://www.lauckgroup.com/main.html

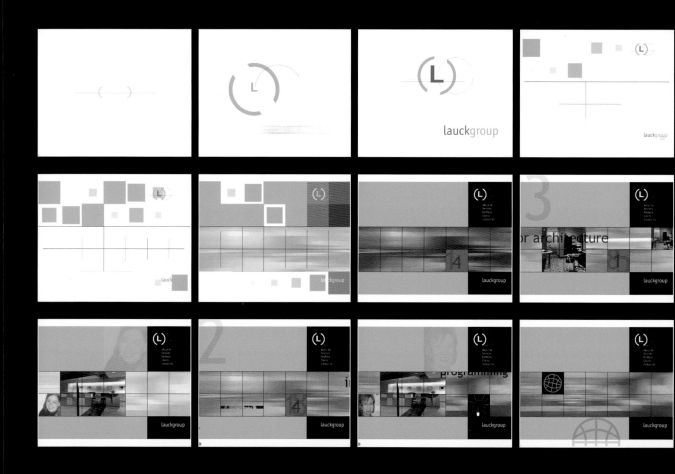

グラフィックデザイン＆インテリア建築／**Graphic Design & Interior Architecture**　**USA**

アメリカはテキサス州にあるインテリア、建築のデザイン会社「lauckgroup」。派手さやパンチはないが、緻密でセンシティヴなフラッシュを見ることができる。また、従業員のポートレイトがスクロールしたり、奇妙なダンスがあったりで遊び心にも楽しさあり。

Lauckgroup is an interior and architectural design firm located in Texas, U.S.A. The Web site is not showy or punchy, but utilizes Flash in a detailed and sensitive way. Scrolling through employee portraits, and an odd dance show, provide enjoyable entertainment.

Soft ware : A, B-1, B-2, M, P	CL : lauckgroup	DF : lauckgroup

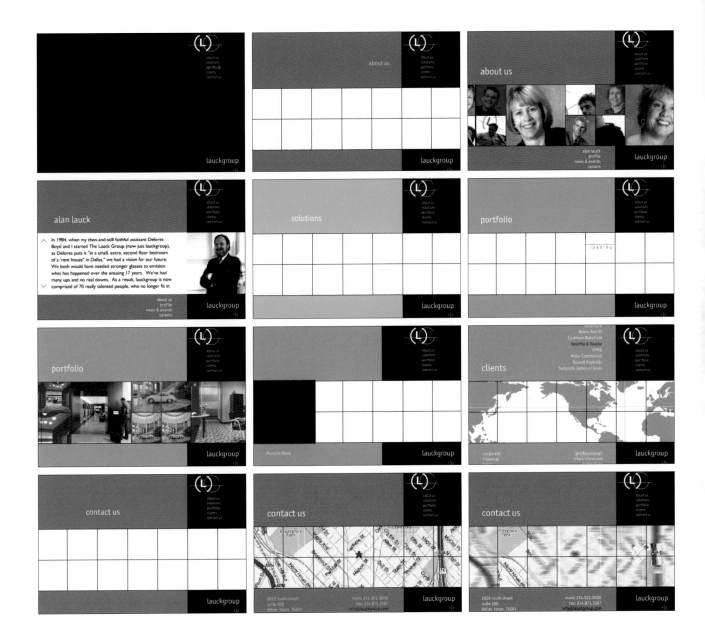

design stage continue

http://www.continue.gr.jp

ウェブサイトデザイン／Website Design　　JAPAN

デザインステージ・コンティニュのサイト。メタリックを基調にしたインターフェースを中心にコンテンツが広がる。デザイナーのサイトだがテキストベースのコラムやHOW TOのページも充実。代表の香西さんは専門誌でフラッシュのテクニカルライターもつとめている。

The Web site of Design Stage Continue. Concepts expand via the base metallic interface. Though it is the site of a designer, it contains such rich text content as columns and how-to pages. Mr. Kasai, the president of Continue, is also a technical writer whose articles about Flash techniques appear in specialist magazines.

Soft ware : A　　CL : Design Stage Continue　　DF : Design Stage Continue

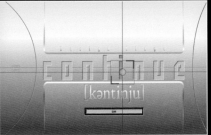

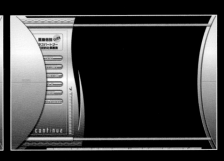

despegar
http://www.mikecesar.com.ar/despegar

旅行業／Travel **ARGENTINA**

旅行会社「Despegar.com」のサイト。アップテンポなモーションとサウンドが小気味良い。飛行交信の声や、飛行機の飛び立つ音が入っていたり、世界地図のまわりを目まぐるしく入れ代わる写真がレイアウトされたりと、世界中を飛び回るイメージが強く感じられる。

Site for the travel agent Despegar.com. The sounds and motions are smart and up tempo. The airborne perspective, control tower voice, and take-off sounds are dizzying. The photo images overlaid on the world map give a strong impression of various destinations.

| Soft ware : A | CL : Despegar.com | DF : Mike Cesar |

rbm

CONSTRUGLOBAL

http://www.mikecesar.com.ar/construglobal

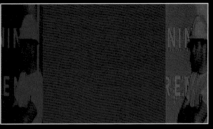  

ARGENTINA   建設業／Construction

建設会社「Construglobal」のサイト。青と黒、赤と黒のダブルトーンで構成された建設現場の写真が、リズミカルなサウンドにのってシャッフルされ、汗臭くないスタイリッシュな躍動感を感じさせる。時折入るノイジーな音が注意を引く。

Site of the construction company "ConstruGlobal." A rhythmical soundtrack accompanies shuffling photos of a construction site in two dual-color schemes-red and black combined with blue and black. The effect gives a throbbing pulse to the text in parentheses, "That is not the stink of sweat." Jarring noises occasionally break in to attract attention.

| Soft ware : A | CL : Construglobal | DF : Mike Cesar |

NON STOP TV

http://www.nonstoptv.com.ar

TV&ケーブル放送制作／TV & Cable Productions　　ARGENTINA

TV&ケーブル放送番組を制作している「Non Stop TV」のサイト。ビビットな色が効いているが、ありがちな激しいモーションではなく、スローでなめらかな動きによって落ち着いた印象を受ける。きれいな画面。

The site for a TV/cable broadcast program produced by NonStop Television. The color accents are effective. You'd expect the dynamic images to have an intense impact, but the fluidity of the movement ends up producing a pleasing, calming effect. The page gets more and more impressive as the seconds tick by. Beautiful screen layout.

Soft ware : A

CL : Non Stop TV

DF : Mike Cesar

ATOMIC Cartoons

http://www.atomiccartoons.com/flash_johnny.html

  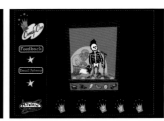 

   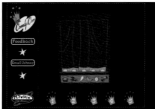

CANADA — アニメーション制作／Animation Production

アニメの制作会社「Atomic Cartoons Inc.」のサイト。エンターテイナーjohnnyのページがおもしろい。ユーザーが彼のパフォーマンスに対するジャッジを下すことができ、それによって彼の身にいろいろな出来事が起こる。ジャッジによって終演のパターンが変わる。

Site of a production company called Atomic Cartoons Inc. This interesting page features a stand-up act by Johnny the comedian. Visitors can clicking on icons to applaud him, heckle him, or even give him diarrhea mid act. There are several versions to the close of Johnny's act, depending on the verdict from the audience.

Soft ware : A	CL : Atomic Cartoons Inc.	DF : Atomic Cartoons Inc.

n.a.s.a.2.0 GmbH
http://www.nasa20.com/vivid

ウェブサイトデザイン／Web Design Agency　　GERMANY

ウェブサイトデザインを手掛ける「n.a.s.a.2.0 GmbH」のサイト。ウェブサイトデザインの会社だけあって、様々なテクノロジーのモーショングラフィックスで構成されている。インタラクティブ要素もふんだんに含まれていて、見応えあり。

Site for the website designer n.a.s.a.2.0 GmbH. This company is dedicated wholly to website design and uses a number of dynamic graphic technologies. An impressive and highly interactive site.

Soft ware : A　　　　CL : n.a.s.a.2.0 GmbH　　　　DF : n.a.s.a.2.0 GmbH

Adam et Ropé '98

2002年3月現在、インターネット上で見ることができません。 As of March 2002, this Website was no longer available.

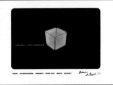 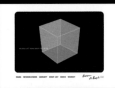  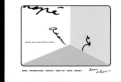 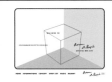

 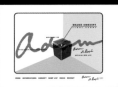 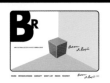  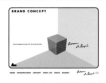

アパレル／Apparel | **JAPAN**

日本のアパレルメーカー「JUN Co.,Ltd.」のブランド「Adam et Ropé」のサイト。毎年、趣向を凝らしたセンスの良いサイトを展開している。美しい色合いが特徴的。

Site for Adam et Ropé, one of the brands under the Japanese apparel maker JUN Co., Ltd. A good sense of the brand's elaborate annual planning is conveyed. The site is unique for its beautiful hue.

Soft ware : A | CL : JUN Co.,Ltd. Adam et Ropé Division | DF : IMAGE DIVE DESIGN OFFICE

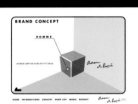

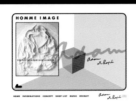

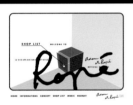

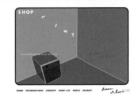

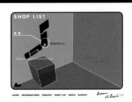

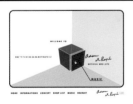

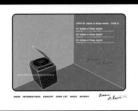

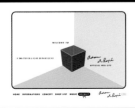

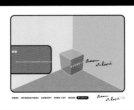

Adam et Ropé '99

2002年3月現在、インターネット上で見ることができません。 As of March 2002, this Website was no longer available.

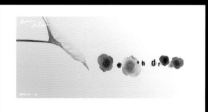

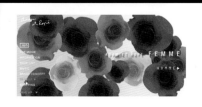

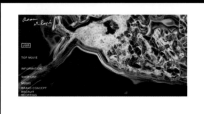

Adam et Ropé '01

2002年3月現在、インターネット上で見ることができません。　As of March,2002, this Website was no longer available.

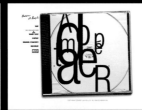

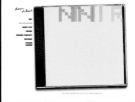

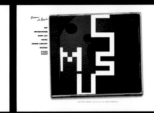

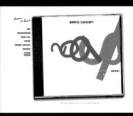

IMAGE DIVE

http://www.imagedive.com

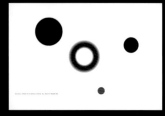   

デザイン事務所／Design Studio **JAPAN**

日本国内において、多くの賞を受賞しているグラフィックデザイン事務所「IMAGE DIVE DESIGN OFFICE」のサイト。美しいグラフィックスに繊細な動きが組み合わさって、ユーザーを魅了する。

Site of the award-winning Japanese design house, Image Dive Design Office. Visitors are charmed by delicate movements coupled with beautiful, crisp graphics.

| Soft ware : A | CL : IMAGE DIVE DESIGN OFFICE | DF : IMAGE DIVE DESIGN OFFICE |

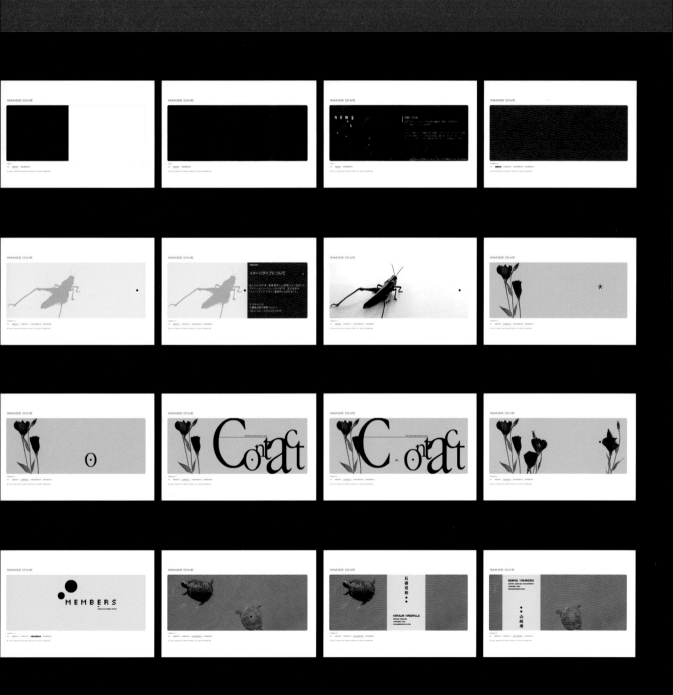

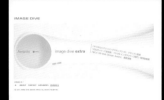

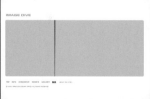

Adam et Ropé '02

http://www.adametrope.com/indexs.html

  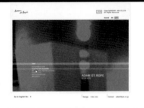 

  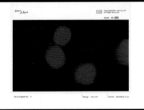 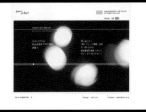

JAPAN アパレル／Apparel

日本のアパレルメーカー「JUN Co.,Ltd.」のブランド「Adam et Ropé」のサイト。スローテンポのサウンドと、イメージグラフィックスがマッチしている。ユーザー参加型の面白い試みとして、e-CardやDMのデザインが体験できるページがある。

Site for Adam et Ropé, one of the brands under the Japanese apparel maker JUN Co., Ltd. The melody and graphics both move at a slow tempo. Visitors can interact in an interesting way with the design of an e-Card and Direct Mail.

| Soft ware : A | CL : JUN Co.,Ltd. Adam et Ropé Division | DF : イメージソース／IMG SRC, INC. |

SONY

http://www.sony.co.jp/

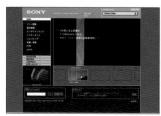   

   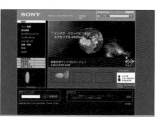

電気機器製造／Electorical Products Manufacturer　　**JAPAN**

日本の電気機器メーカー「SONY」のオフィシャルサイト。フレームが落ち着いた色なので、一見地味に見えてしまうが、逆にそれが製品の写真をクリアで美しく見せている。インタラクティブなモーションもいい。

Official site of the electronics giant Sony. Don't move the cursor, and the page stays mostly still. Move the cursor and everything sets in motion. Frames scroll in different directions and the cursor controls a window that opens up partial views of product photos. The interactive motion is excellent.

| Soft ware : A | CL : SONY | DF：イメージソース／IMG SRC, INC. |

marcnail

http://www.marcnail.com

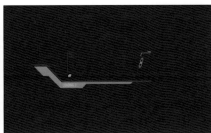
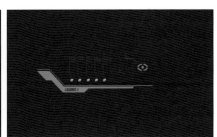

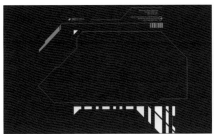
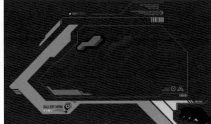

GERMANY ウェブサイトデザイン／**Website Design**

ウェブサイトデザインを手掛ける「pepworks」のサイト。cyobreed THE GAME-SERIESに登場するキャラクターのアートワークを紹介するページ。動き、効果音などが機械的なイメージで近未来を感じさせる。

A site for the website designer pepworks. The pages feature characters and machines from the game cyobreed THE GAME-SERIES. Slick, high-tech sounds and movements enhance the experience of a "mechano" world of the near future.

Soft ware : A, B-2, P	CL : pepworks	DF : pepworks

7ate9.tv

http://www.7ate9.tv

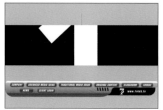   

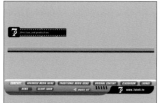  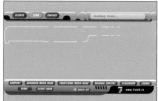 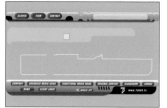

映画＆DVD制作／Film & DVD Producer　　GERMANY

映画＆DVDを制作している「7ate9.tv」のサイト。フィルムが流れていくイメージのモーションで、数字がカウントされながら7と9が組み合わさって7ate9.tvのロゴマークとなるのはおもしろい。大げさな効果音が機械を取扱っているような感覚にさせる。

Site for 7ate9.tv, a producer of commercial films and DVDs. Digits fly across the frame, starting from one and counting up. Just after 7 appears, it eats up 9 and the graphic morphs into the "7ate9" logo. The droning, aggressive sound gives a machine-like effect to the rapid-flash succession of images in the central frame.

Soft ware : A, B-2, G-1　　　　CL : 7ate9. tv　　　　DF : pepworks

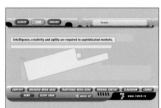

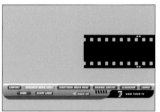
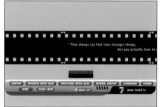
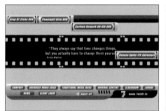

WireFlame

http://www.wireflame.com

 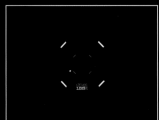 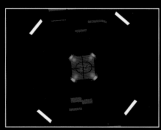 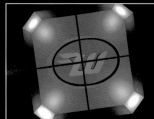

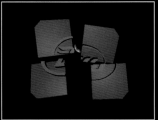   

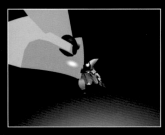 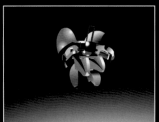  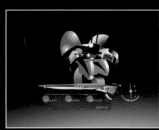

ウェブサイトデザイン／**Website Design** **GERMANY**

多くのウェブサイトデザインを手掛ける「pepworks」のサイト。暗い空間の光のトンネルを抜けて、まるでコンピューターゲームをしているように進んでいく。ナビゲーター役のロボットの動きがいい。

Another site for the website designer pepworks.com. As the page loads, visitors are passed through space in a tunnel of light, as if they were in a game. The robot for page navigation moves nicely.

Soft ware : A, B-2, E-3, P | CL : wireflame / pepworks | DF : wireflame / pepworks

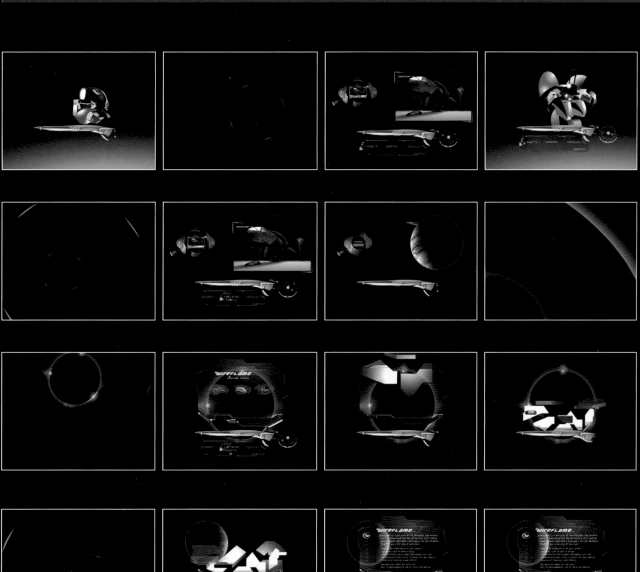

3D groove

http://www.3dgroove.com

 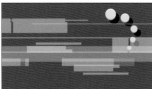  

3Dゲーム開発／3D Games Developer　　**GERMANY**

3Dゲームを開発している「3dgroove」のサイト。ポーズを変えないキャラクターのシルエットと3Dgrooveのロゴが所狭しと動き回るポップなモーショングラフィックス。

Site for the 3D game developer 3dgroove. Fast-moving graphics. The logotype, the cut-out silhouette of two gun-wielding women with afros, careens all over the screen.

| Soft ware : A, B-2, P | CL : 3dgroove | DF : pepworks |

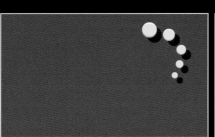
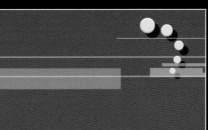

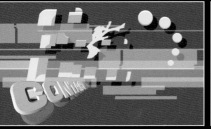
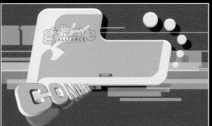

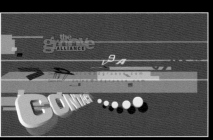

THE cyobreed GAME-SERIES

http://www.pepworks.com/

ウェブサイトデザイン／Website Design　　**GERMANY**

多くのウェブサイトデザインを手掛ける「pepworks」のサイト。若干、ぎこちない動きをする場面もあるが、TVでアニメ番組を見ているような手の込んだグラフィックス。他のページにもモーショングラフィックスが満載されている。

The site for the website designer pepworks. The images come together before your eyes in a TV-like frame. The opening page is less dynamic than the pages that follow.

| Soft ware : A, B-2, P | CL : pepworks | DF : pepworks |

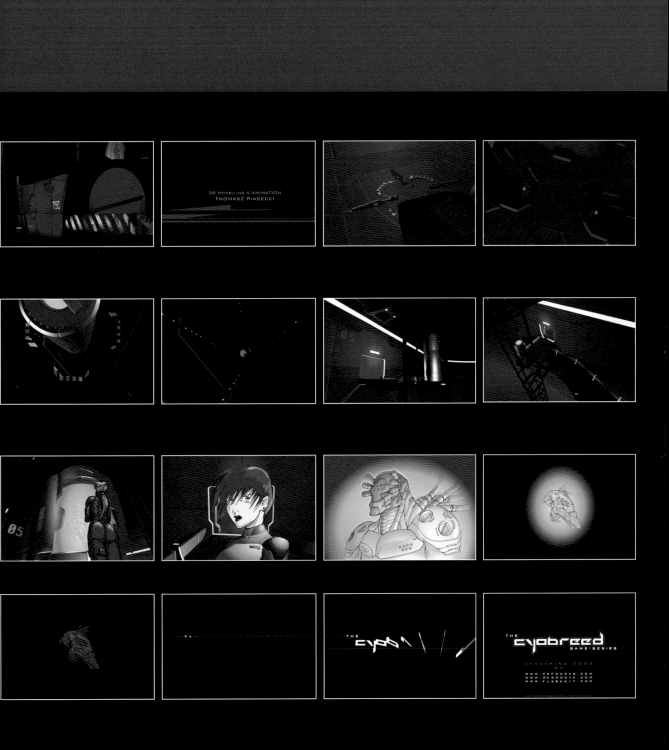

INDEPENDENCE

http://www.independence-cigar.de/

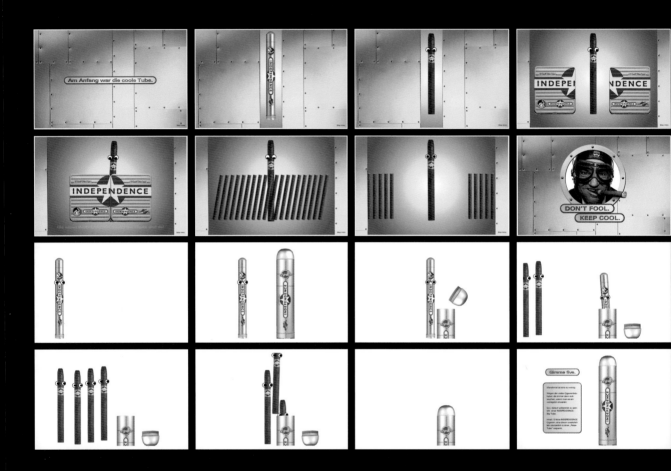

はまき製造／Tobacco Company   GERMANY

はまきを製造している「Arnold André-The Ciger Company」のサイト。はまき達が様々なパフォーマンスをして、大いに楽しませてくれる。サウンドも効いている。

Site for Arnold André Cigars. A cigar-shaped character puts on an excellent performance. The sounds are also effective.

Soft ware : A, B-2, B-3, G-3, P   CL : Arnold André-The Ciger Company   DF : Rullkötter AGD

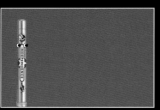  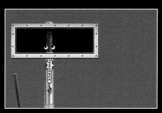 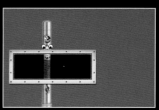

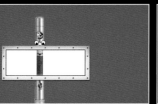   

MIGHTY ASSEMBLY

http://www.mightyassembly.com

   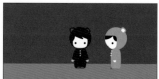

オンスクリーン デザインスタジオ／Onscreen design studio ▶ **USA**

オンスクリーンデザインを手掛けている「Mighty Assembly」のサイト。動きに、なんとも言えない不思議な間があり、独自の雰囲気を醸し出している。

Site for Mighty Assembly, an "onscreen design studio." Visitors extract information by clicking on a small grouping of gear-like scrolls positioned at the center of the screen. Original and quirky, with robotic synth sounds.

Soft ware : A, B-1, B-2, D-1, G-2, G-4, H-1, H-2, I, J, K, L   CL : Mighty Assembly   DF : Mighty Assembly

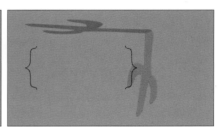

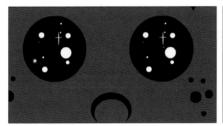

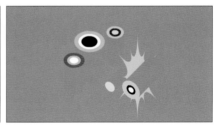

>> **MIGHTY ASSEMBLY**

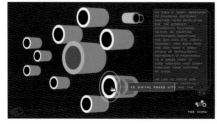
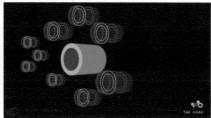

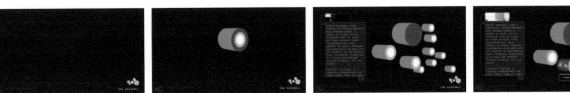
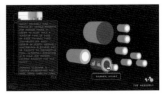

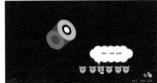

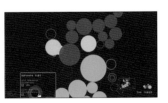

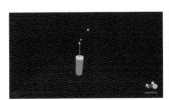

OmniSky
http://www.omniskywireless.com/

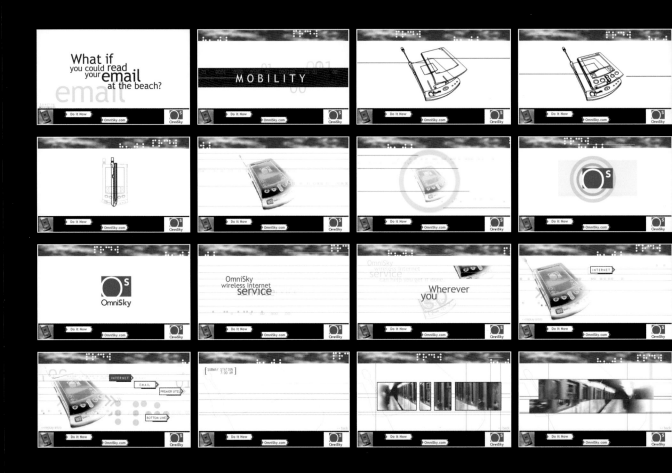

インターネットプロバイダー／Internet Service Provider　　USA

インターネットプロバイダー「OmniSky」のサイト。軽快なサウンドにのって、モバイルの使用例をモーショングラフィックスで紹介している。

Site for the Internet provider OmniSky. American mainstream style. Light "pitter-patter" soundtrack with dynamic images of device schematics, slogans, and users going online with their handhelds.

Soft ware : A　　　　　CL : OmniSky　　　　　DF : JUXT Interactive

BILLABONG

http://www.billabong-usa.com/billabong_set.cfm?section=home

スポーツウェア製造・販売／Sportswear Manufacture & Sales | **USA**

エクストリームスポーツの用品を中心に展開しているメーカー「Billabong USA」のサイト。極限に挑戦する選手たちの勇姿が印象的。多くのグラフィックが重なり更にモーションも重なるので、少し目がチラつく感もある。

Site for Billabong USA, the sporting goods maker specialized in "extreme" sports. Fearless punks doing hairy stunts on skateboards and snowboards. The pages are packed with lots of rapid-fire graphics. Motion conflicts are set up to create a jerky, jarring visual experience.

Soft ware : A | CL : Billabong USA | DF : JUXT Interactive

Ultrashock

  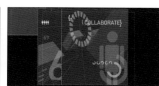 

USA 情報サイト／Online Resource Site

情報サイト「Ultrashock.com」。派手な展開ではないが、凝った作り。際限ない空間を情報が飛び交っているイメージだろうか？見始めは少し地味でおとなしいが、途中からサウンドと共にアップテンポになり気分も乗ってくる。

An information site run by Ultrashock.com. Not a showy site, but one elaborate in the making. Why is the information flying around in space? Calming in the beginning and up tempo from the middle, with building feeling in the soundtrack.

Soft ware : A

CL : Ultrashock.com

DF : JUXT Interactive

PICKLED.TV

http://www.pickled.tv/main.html

  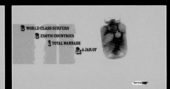 

スポーツウェア製造・販売／Sportswear Manufacture & Sales　　USA

エクストリームスポーツウェアメーカー「Billabong USA」のサイト。マスタード色の背景に、ピクルスの入ったビンやグラスの写真がレイアウトされ
え、いったい何のサイトだか分かりづらいが、インパクトがある。

Another site by Billabong USA, the sporting goods maker specialized in "extreme" sports. A bottle. A mustard-colored photo of pickles going into a glass in the background. Incomprehensible? Very. The impact lies in the question: "What on earth is this site?"

| Soft ware : A | CL : Billabong USA | DF : JUXT Interactive |

FLASH deCONSTRUCTION

http://juxtinteractive.com/deCONSTRUCTION/deconstruction_set.html

FLASH

FLASH deCONSTRUCTION

FLASH deCONSTRUCTION

FLASH deCONSTRUCTION

FLASH deCONSTRUCTION

FLASH deCONSTRUCTION

FLASH deCONSTRUCTION

FLASH deCONSTRUCTION

USA 出版／Publisher

出版社「New Riders Press」のサイト。カーソルが自動的に動き回り、次々とページレイアウトを完成させていく。不思議な形に切り抜かれた写真も良いバランスで美しい。

Site by the publishing company New Riders Press. The cursor moves all by itself, changing the page layout in sequence. A beautiful photographic texture adds good balance.

Soft ware : A	CL : New Riders Press	DF : JUXT Interactive

JAM: Tokyo London Exhibition

http://www.onlinejam.co.uk

   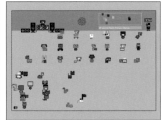

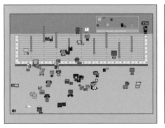   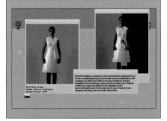

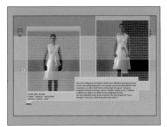 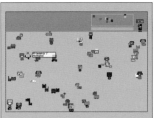 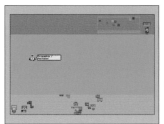 

アートギャラリー／Fine Art Gallery   UK

アートギャラリー「JAM: Tokyo London Exhibition」のサイト。鮮やかな色使いで、コンテンツボタンでもあるポップでかわいいキャラクターたちが
あちこち動き回る。赤ん坊をあやす時に聞かせるような音楽もマッチしている。

A promotional site for an art exhibit, the JAM: Tokyo London Exhibition. Blocky cartoon figures drift over vivid colors and an occasional content button.
The cuddly, naive music matches the visuals well.

Soft ware : A, B-2, K, O-1, P   CL : JAM: Tokyo London Exhibition   DF : Airside

WHITE CUBE

http://www.whitecube.com

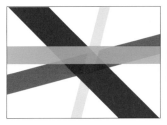  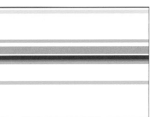 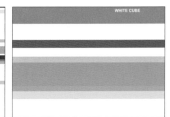

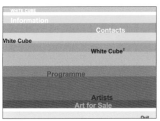   

UK / アートギャラリー／Fine Art Gallery

アートギャラリー「White Cube Gallery」のサイト。イントロで、軽快なサウンドにのってカラーのラインが交差し、トップ画面である重なりあった色の帯に変化していくモーションが美しい。

Site for the White Cube Gallery. Begins with light sounds and intersecting colored lines, then the lines change into colored zones that overlap each other and eventually fill the entire screen.

Soft ware : A, B-2, K, O-1, P	CL : White Cube Gallery	DF : Airside

higher source
http://www.highersourcemusic.com/

 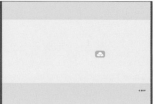  

レコード＆グッズ販売／Records & Gear Retailer　**USA**

レコードとその関連グッズを販売している「Higher Source Music」のサイト。派手ではないが、色を抑えているところがかえってかっこいい。ピクトグラムがふんだんに使われいてクールでポップなイメージ。

Site for Higher Source Music, a specialty retailer for DJ goods. Not showy at the beginning. Rapid-fire images flash across the screen, but not a hurried feeling. Heavy use of pictograms and a subdued color scheme. The staccato drumbeat matches the images.

Soft ware : A	CL : Higher Source Music	DF : 2Advanced Studios

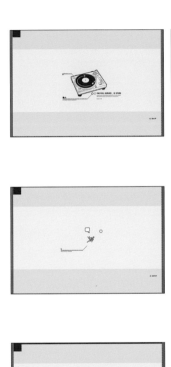

create online

http://www.2advanced.com/createonline/

  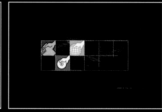 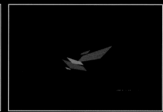

  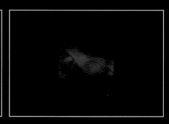 

ウェブマガジン／Website Magazine   USA

ウェブマガジン「CreateOnline Magazine」を紹介するサイト。ブラックをベースに敷いた画面に赤色を用いたグラフィックスが栄える。軽快なサウンドと要所要所に入る効果音が意識を集中させる。

A site introducing CreateOnline Magazine. The red for the graphics works beautifully against the black background. The light sound effects frame the flashing visuals, focusing the viewer's attention and adding impact.

| Soft ware : A | CL : CreateOnline Magazine | DF : 2Advanced Studios |

VULCAN

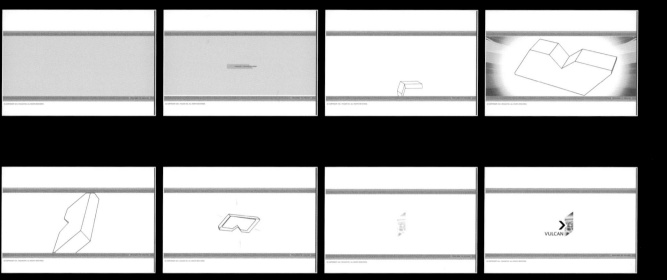

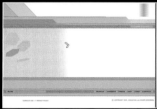

USA　ベンチャー企業／Venture Capital Holding Company

ベンチャー企業「Vulcan, Inc.」のサイト。すっきりシンプルな画面構成でとても見やすい。Vulcan, Inc.のイメージマークが曲芸飛行機の様に飛び交い、最終的に合体することで、後から現れる会社名のロゴをを印象付けるのに役立っている。

Site for venture business called Vulcan, Inc. A simple screen composition with a hierarchical menu structure gives a good feeling of stability. The Vulcan logo flies around like a stunt machine, then the company name pops up and sidles up to the graphic. Frenetic motion settles down to a stable corporate logo.

Soft ware : A	CL : Vulcan, Inc.	DF : 2Advanced Studios

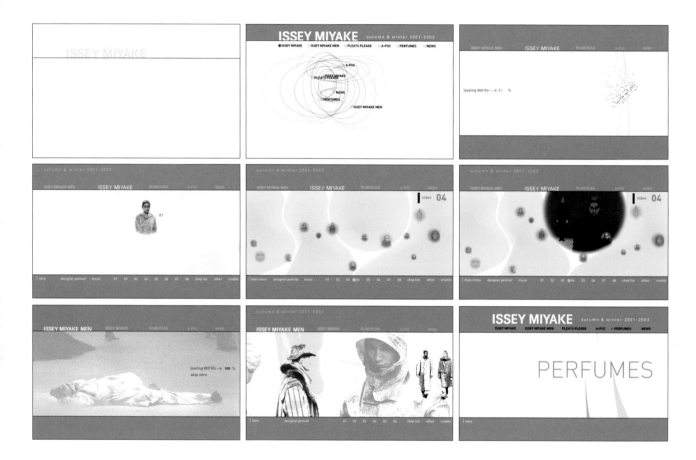

ISSEY MIYAKE
http://www.isseymiyake.com

アパレル／Apparel JAPAN

アパレルブランド「イッセイ ミヤケ」のオフィシャルサイト。静寂の世界で、ぼんやりとした写真と、ゆったり動くモーショングラフィックスが独自のブランドイメージを作り出している。

Official site for the apparel brand, Issey Miyake. Pass the cursor over the quietly scrolling catwalk and watch color photographs softly grow. Calm, quiet, lingering. An original brand image.

| Soft ware : A, B-1, B-2 | CL : イッセイ ミヤケ／ISSEY MIYAKE INC. | DF : Incandescence.com |

LEVEL RED

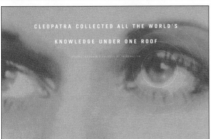

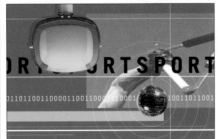

USA / インタラクティブ・エンターテインメント／Interactive Entertainment

インタラクティブ・エンターテインメントを創造している「LEVEL RED」のサイト。メリハリのある展開、ハッキリした色使いなので、かなり目立つ。内容も分かりやすい。

Site for a an interactive entertainment company, LEVEL RED. Pure solid colors, simple shapes, stable pace. Short text messages. Clear, memorable information delivery.

| Soft ware : A, B-2, B-3 | CL : LEVEL RED | DF : HOLLIS |

HOLLIS

http://www.hollisdesign.com

  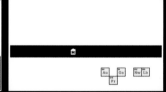 

ブランド戦略／Band Strategy　USA

ブランド戦略を展開している「HOLLIS」のサイト。爆弾が破裂するところから始まる面白いサイト。色や効果音、コンテンツボタンを押した時の反応など、全てにおいてメリハリがあって良い。

Site for HOLLIS, a brand strategy developer. Interesting from the very beginning. Click the enter button and a bomb will blast you into the main menu page.　Good control of color, sound effects, and content buttons.

Soft ware : A, B-2, B-3	CL : HOLLIS	DF : HOLLIS

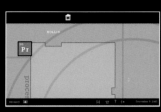

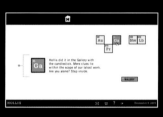

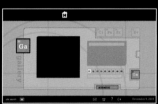

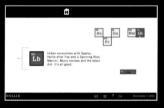

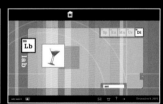

The Jerusalem Archaeological Park

http://www.archpark.org.il/

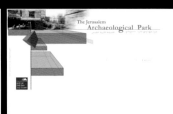

政府機関／Government Agency   ISRAEL

イスラエルの古代遺物に関わる政府機関「Israel Antiquities Authority」のサイト。年代別の古代遺物を紹介するページでは、事前に検索方法の説明まで付いていて親切。

Site for the Jerusalem Archeological Park, run by the Israel government's Antiquities Authority. Worlds of yesterday remain today. A guide through generations of history, with thorough text explanations and a wonderful, easy-to-navigate timeline.

Soft ware : A, B-2, B-3, G-1, Q-2   CL : Israel Antiquities Authority   DF : Eagleshade Interactive Production House

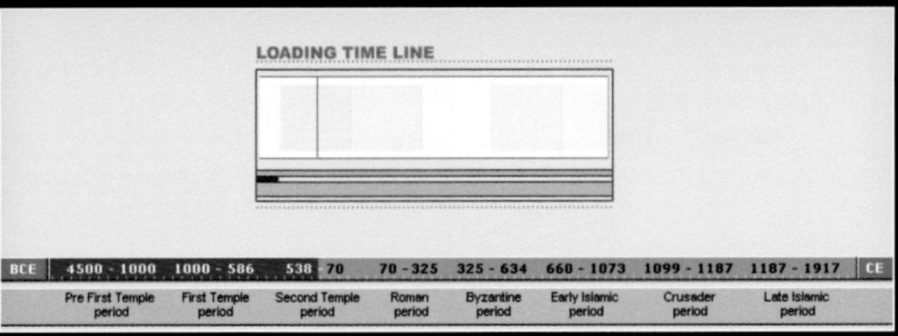
LOADING TIME LINE
BCE 4500 - 1000 1000 - 586 538 70 70 - 325 325 - 634 660 - 1073 1099 - 1187 1187 - 1917 CE
Pre First Temple period
First Temple period
Second Temple period
Roman period
Byzantine period
Early Islamic period
Crusader period
Late Islamic period

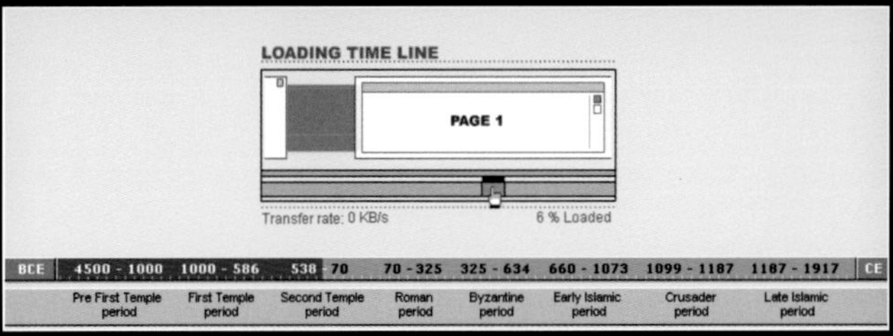
LOADING TIME LINE
PAGE 1
Transfer rate: 0 KB/s
6 % Loaded
BCE 4500 - 1000 1000 - 586 538 70 70 - 325 325 - 634 660 - 1073 1099 - 1187 1187 - 1917 CE
Pre First Temple period
First Temple period
Second Temple period
Roman period
Byzantine period
Early Islamic period
Crusader period
Late Islamic period

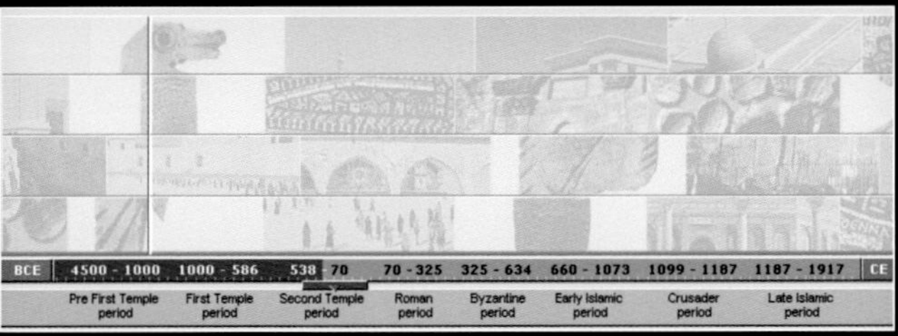
BCE 4500 - 1000 1000 - 586 538 70 70 - 325 325 - 634 660 - 1073 1099 - 1187 1187 - 1917 CE
Pre First Temple period
First Temple period
Second Temple period
Roman period
Byzantine period
Early Islamic period
Crusader period
Late Islamic period

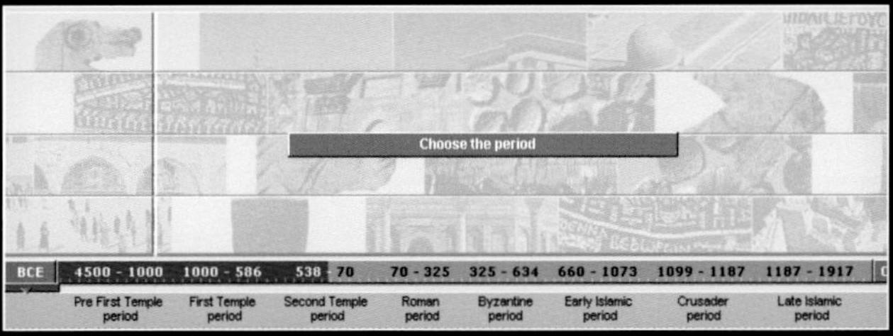
Choose the period
BCE 4500 - 1000 1000 - 586 538 70 70 - 325 325 - 634 660 - 1073 1099 - 1187 1187 - 1917
Pre First Temple period
First Temple period
Second Temple period
Roman period
Byzantine period
Early Islamic period
Crusader period
Late Islamic period

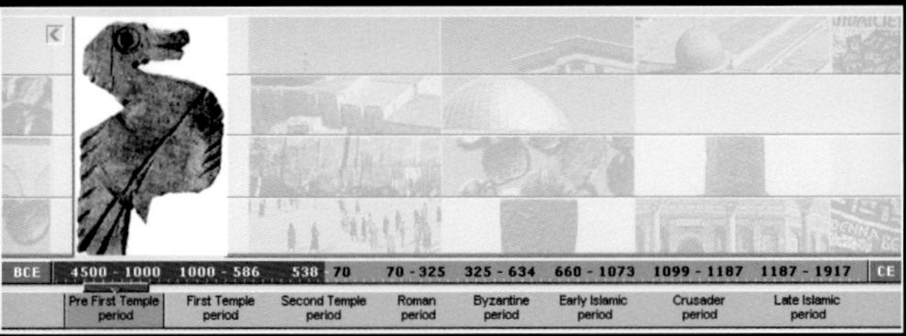
BCE 4500 - 1000 1000 - 586 538 70 70 - 325 325 - 634 660 - 1073 1099 - 1187 1187 - 1917 CE
Pre First Temple period
First Temple period
Second Temple period
Roman period
Byzantine period
Early Islamic period
Crusader period
Late Islamic period

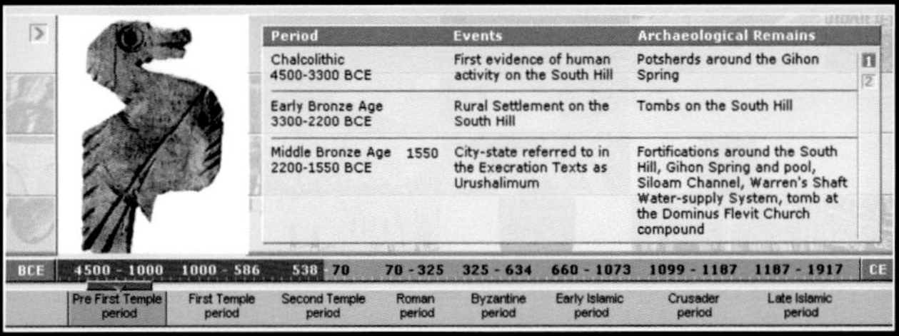
Period
Events
Archaeological Remains
Chalcolithic 4500-3300 BCE
First evidence of human activity on the South Hill
Potsherds around the Gihon Spring
Early Bronze Age 3300-2200 BCE
Rural Settlement on the South Hill
Tombs on the South Hill
Middle Bronze Age 2200-1550 BCE
1550
City-state referred to in the Execration Texts as Urushalimum
Fortifications around the South Hill, Gihon Spring and pool, Siloam Channel, Warren's Shaft Water-supply System, tomb at the Dominus Flevit Church compound
BCE 4500 - 1000 1000 - 586 538 70 70 - 325 325 - 634 660 - 1073 1099 - 1187 1187 - 1917 CE
Pre First Temple period
First Temple period
Second Temple period
Roman period
Byzantine period
Early Islamic period
Crusader period
Late Islamic period

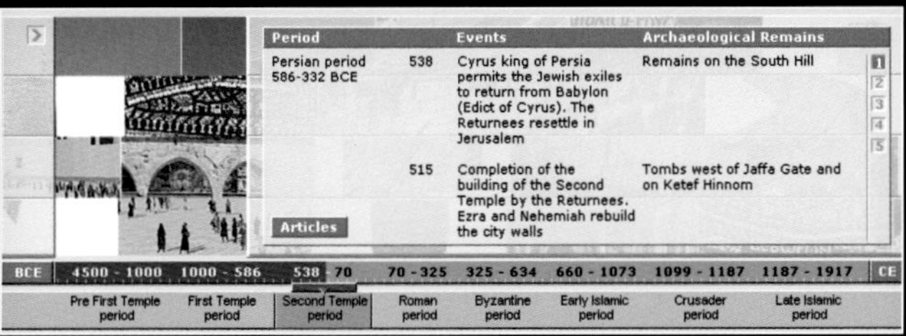
Period
Events
Archaeological Remains
Persian period 586-332 BCE
538
Cyrus king of Persia permits the Jewish exiles to return from Babylon (Edict of Cyrus). The Returnees resettle in Jerusalem
Remains on the South Hill
515
Completion of the building of the Second Temple by the Returnees. Ezra and Nehemiah rebuild the city walls
Tombs west of Jaffa Gate and on Ketef Hinnom
Articles
BCE 4500 - 1000 1000 - 586 538 70 70 - 325 325 - 634 660 - 1073 1099 - 1187 1187 - 1917 CE
Pre First Temple period
First Temple period
Second Temple period
Roman period
Byzantine period
Early Islamic period
Crusader period
Late Islamic period

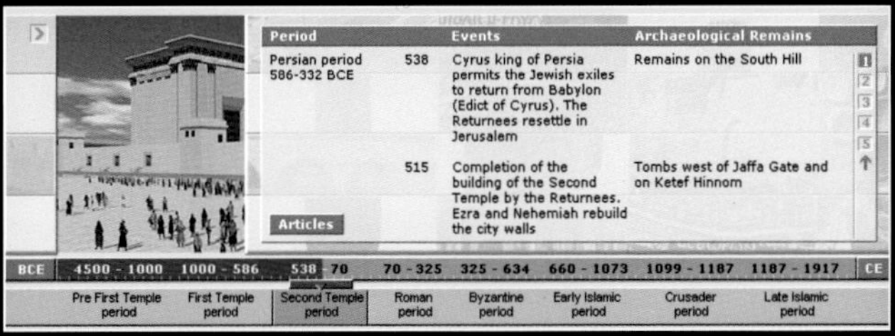
Period
Events
Archaeological Remains
Persian period 586-332 BCE
538
Cyrus king of Persia permits the Jewish exiles to return from Babylon (Edict of Cyrus). The Returnees resettle in Jerusalem
Remains on the South Hill
515
Completion of the building of the Second Temple by the Returnees. Ezra and Nehemiah rebuild the city walls
Tombs west of Jaffa Gate and on Ketef Hinnom
Articles
BCE 4500 - 1000 1000 - 586 538 70 70 - 325 325 - 634 660 - 1073 1099 - 1187 1187 - 1917 CE
Pre First Temple period
First Temple period
Second Temple period
Roman period
Byzantine period
Early Islamic period
Crusader period
Late Islamic period

EAGLESHADE INTERACTIVE PRODUCTION HOUSE

http://www.eagleshade.com

インタラクティブ・デザイン／Interactive Design　　**ISRAEL**

イスラエルのインタラクティブ・デザイン事務所「Eagleshade Interactive Production House」のサイト。ドラマ仕立てのアニメーション。シャドー部分をうまく使っていて、おもしろい。

Site of the Israeli interactive design office, Eagleshade Interactive Production House. A dramatic cartoon with skillful and interesting use of shadows.

| Soft ware : A, B-2, B-3, G-1, Q-2 | CL : Eagleshade Interactive Production House | DF : Eagleshade Interactive Production House |

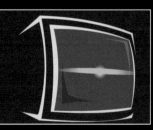

Presentation

Coca-Cola
http://www.coca-cola.com

 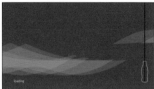  

  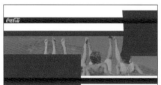 

飲料製造／Beverage Manufacturer　　**USA**

世界的に有名なノンアルコール飲料「Coca-Cola」のオフィシャルサイト。イメージカラーである赤色を、随所に使用した印象に残るサイト。トップ画面のふわふわ浮いている丸いコンテンツボタンにカーソルを合わせると、雫が滴り落ちる。

Official site of the global soda pop behemoth Coca-Cola. The flagship Coca-Cola red fills up just about every part of every page on the site. Pass the cursor over one of the floating, planet-shaped windows, and the window pops forward with a liquid effect.

Soft ware : A　　　　CL : The Coca-Cola Company　　　　DF : Zentropy Partners

 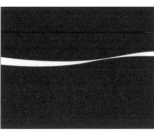  

MJF

http://www.mjf.co.uk/

業務環境コンサルタント／Workspace Consultants　UK

業務環境コンサルタントの会社「MJF」のサイト。水色を基調とした、シンプルですっきり見やすいレイアウト。小さな立方体が動いて何種類かの図形を形成していく。

Site for the "business environment" consultant MJF. A simple tone and layout, with a "good-feeling" light blue. The visitor's attention is drawn directly to the center of the screen, where two groups of small cubes float around in chaos.

Soft ware : A　　　CL : MJF　　　DF : Tonic

etc.

http://www.etc-uk.com

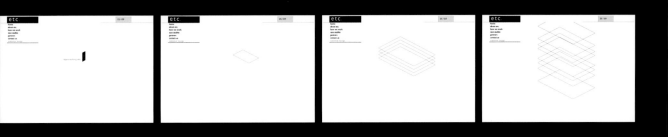

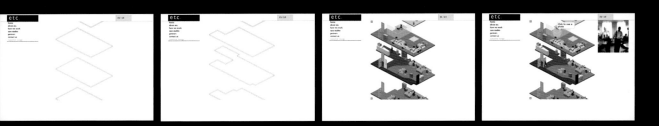

業務環境コンサルタントの会社「etc.」のサイト。トップ画面にオフィスの階層毎フロアマップが配置され、各ポイントの業務環境を、写真やコメントで知ることができる。

The site for etc., another "business environment" consultant. The four floors of an office are mapped out in detail and stacked up. Click on a spot on a map, and a detailed photo of the scene appears on the upper right with a text comment.

Soft ware : N　　　CL : etc.　　　DF : Tonic

Volkswagen

http://www.volkswagen.co.uk/

自動車製造／Automobile Manufacturer　　UK

自動車メーカー「Volkswagen」のサイト。色帯によるグラデーションと写真の組み合わせが美しい。落ち着いたレイアウトで、上質なイメージが感じ取れる。

Volkswagen's UK site. Click one of a series of gradated color zones and watch it expand to a beautiful photo or image with a sub-menu. Once the movement stops, the "good quality" image hits home.

| Soft ware : A | CL : Volkswagen | DF : Tonic |

Tonic

http://www.tonic.co.uk/

UK デザイン・コンサルタント／**Design Consultancy**

多くのデザインを手掛けているデザインコンサルタント会社「Tonic」のサイト。Tonicが作るウェブサイトデザインは色使いの美しさ、レイアウトの見やすさ、上品さが特徴。

A refined site by a design consultant called Tonic. Distinguished by the beauty of its colors, a readily understandable layout, and a semi-interactive task set up for the visitor.

Soft ware : A | CL : Tonic | DF : Tonic

Presentation

GUCCI

http://www.gucci.com/start.html

ファッション／Fashion **USA**

ファッションブランド「GUCCI」のサイト。ブラックを基調とした引き締まった画面。ぼんやり暗い中からモデルの写真が浮かび上がってくる様はまるで、ファッションショー会場で、モデルがステージを歩いてくる感覚。

Site of the luxury brand GUCCI. A photo of a fashion model walking on stage emerges from an all-black screen, expanding into a full-screen fashion show scene.

Soft ware : A, B-1, B-2, K	CL : Gucci Group	DF : Method

THE APARTMENT

http://www.theapt.com/flash/theapt.html

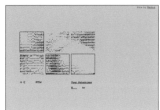

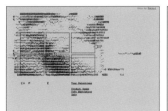

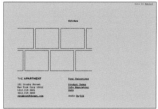

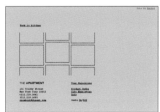

USA 家具＆インテリアデザインストア／Furniture & Design Store

家具＆インテリアデザインストア「The Apartment」のサイト。ノイジーなオープニングから展開し、各部屋を監視カメラで見ているような少し粗い画像のムービーがレイアウトされている。覗き見的な感覚で、商品のチェックができる。

Site for a New York furniture and interior design retailer called The Apartment. Set up like a video surveillance system for an apartment. The opening screen starts with six frames, each with a low-resolution image of a room. Click on any room, and six scenes inside the room pop up, complete with the live-in couple doing personal things. Click again and see actual merchandise. Excellent soundtrack with jazzy music and static fuzz.

Soft ware : B-1, B-2, D-3, K, L, O-2, R   CL : The Apartment   DF : Method

FULL THROTTLE
http://www.davidgarystudios.com/

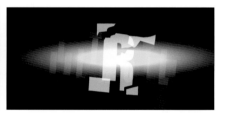

デザイン事務所／Design Studio　　**USA**

デザイン事務所「David Gary Studio」のサイト。サイト名が「FULL THROTTLE」というだけあって、イントロからバイクのスロットルを吹かす音が響く。トップページではロボットが金属音を発しながら作動する。見応えのあるモーショングラフィックス。

Site for David Gary Studio, a design office. A futuristic robot assembles itself on screen and provides a FULL THROTTLE that you can rev up like a motorcycle. Outstanding graphics and sound.

Soft ware : A	CL : David Gary Studio	DF : David Gary Studio

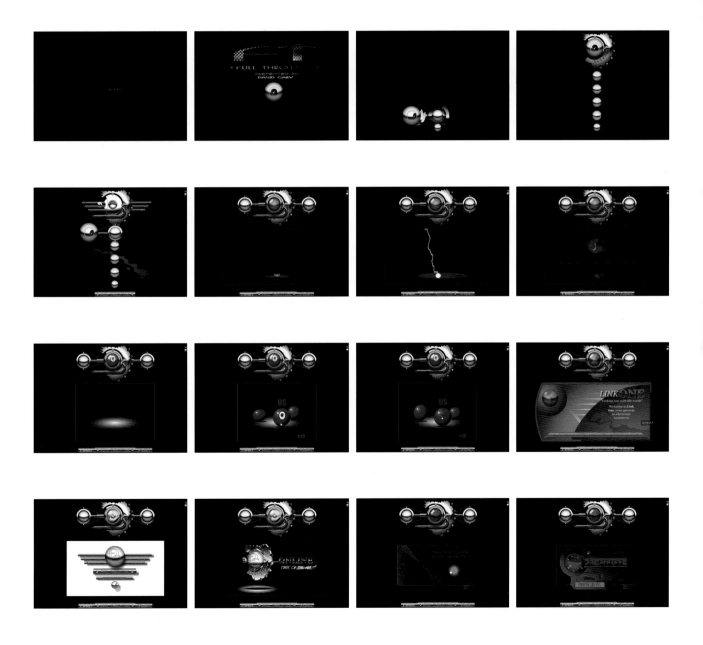

WM TEAM

http://www.wmteam.de

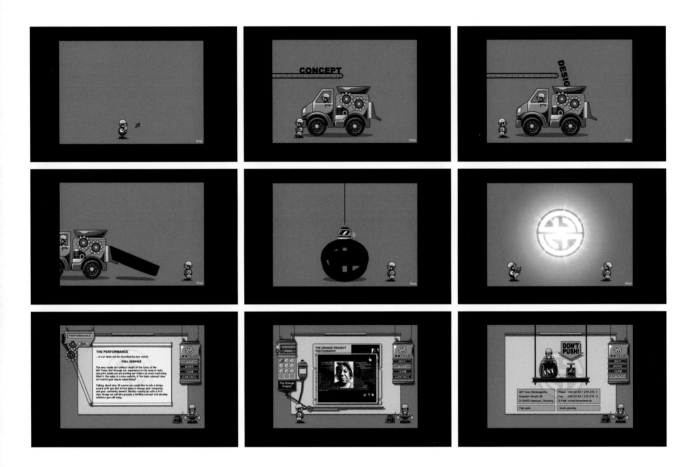

広告代理店／Advertising Agency　　GERMANY

広告代理店「wm team」のサイト。コミカルな作業員のキャラクターがナビゲート。彼らの動きを見ているだけで楽しくなる。何げにたばこを吸ったり、ラジカセで音楽を鳴らしてみたり、細かい所まで気の効いたサイトだ。

Site for the advertising agency wm team. A couple of animated construction workers guide you through the site. They smoke and try to play music on their portable stereo. A light-spirited site suitable for a smaller company.

Soft ware : A, B-2, B-3　　　　CL : wm team　　　　DF : wm team

Strawberryfrog

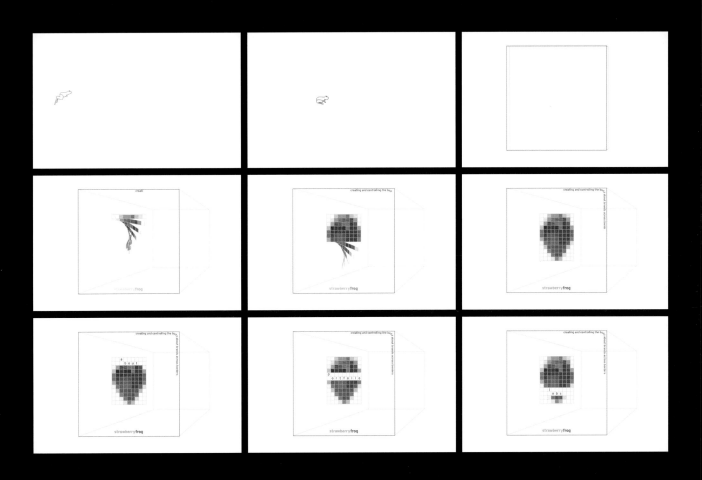

広く、広告代理業やマーケティングを行っている「StrawberryFrog」のサイト。イントロで出てくるカエルの動きがいい感じ。パネルで出来たイチゴの動きの旋律が美しい。

The site for StrawberryFrog, an advertising and marketing agency. The hopping frog at the intro is good. The movement of the frog at the intro is good, and the melodious movement of the mosaic strawberry is beautiful.

Soft ware : A	CL : StrawberryFrog	DF : The Void New Media

SALOMON (FALL WINTER 2000)

http://www.salomonoutdoor.com

  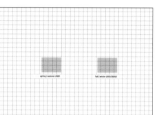 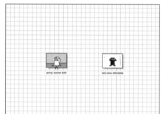

 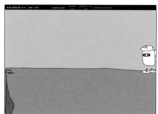  

 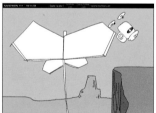  

スポーツ用品製造・販売／Sports company　**FRANCE**

フランスのスポーツグッズメーカー「SALOMON」のオフィシャルサイト。愛嬌があり、ちょっとぽけた感じのキャラクターが、様々なスポーツにチャレンジしていて楽しい。

Official site for the French sporting goods maker Salomon. An amiable, nonchalant approach to sports. The characters seem to dig sports, but feign ignorance about them at the same time. A cheering site.

Soft ware : A, B-2, Q-1　　　　CL : SALOMON　　　　DF : MEGALOSTUDIO

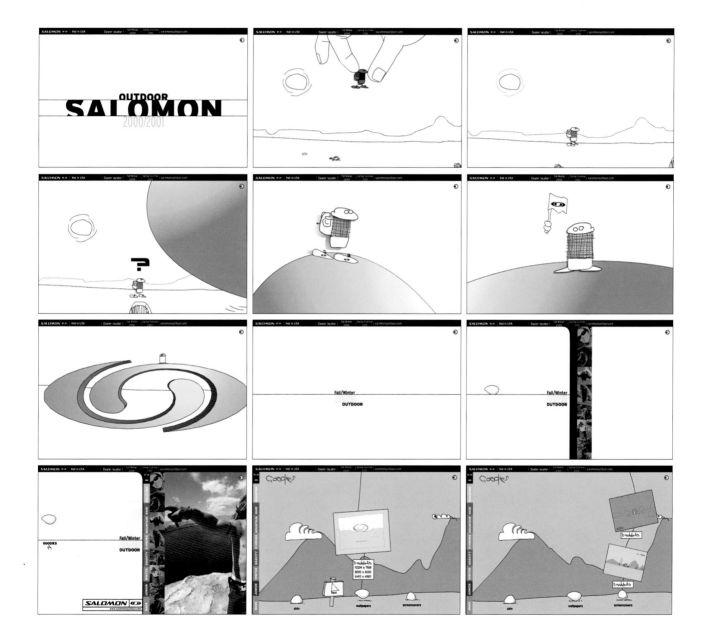

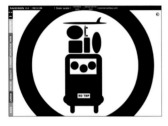

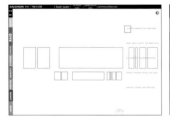

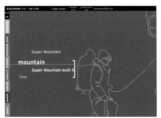

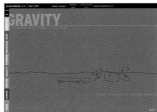

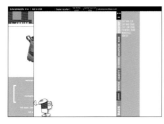

SALOMON (SPRING SUMMER 2001)

http://www.salomonoutdoor.com

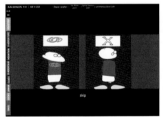

FARMHOUSE

http://www.phish.com/farmhouse/index_flash.html

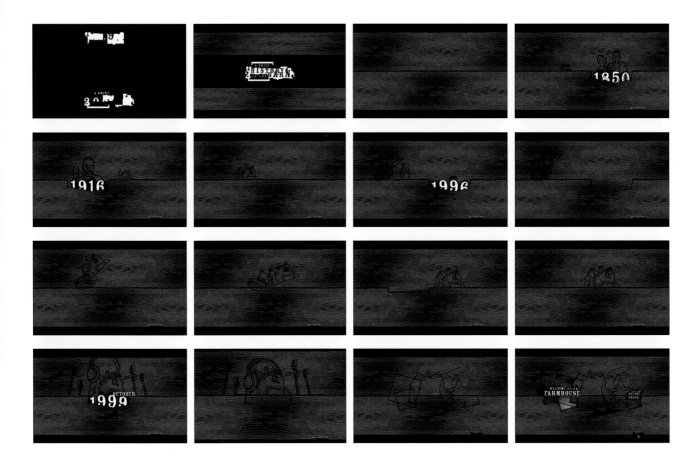

ロックバンド／Rock Band　**USA**

ロックバンド「Phish」のサイト。ブルーグレーの木目柄の上を、筆描きのようなイラストが独自のテンポで動いていく。色調が極めてダークで、なんとも言えない不思議な雰囲気である。

The farmhouse site for the rock band Phish. The brush-like illustrations move in sync with a Phish song along the bare grain of a couple of wooden planks in blue gray. The images fill with color and darkness, creating a mysterious mood.

Soft ware : A	CL : Phish	DF : The Chopping Block

http://www.colal.pt

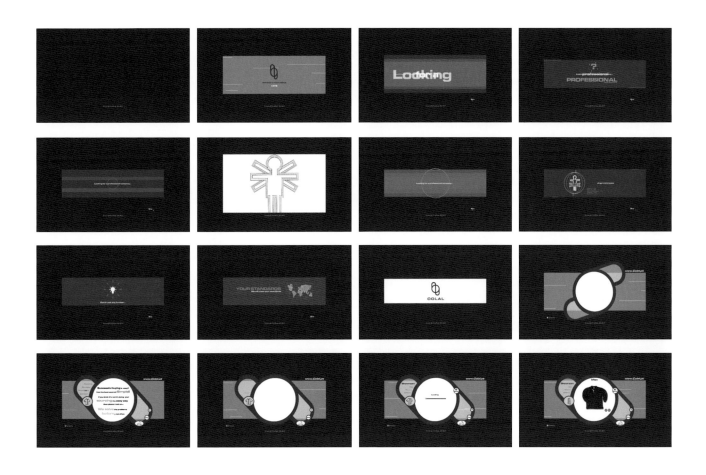

PORTUGAL 服飾縫製／Sourcing company

ポルトガルのウエアブランド、COLALのオフィシャルサイト。テクノを使用したスピード感溢れるオープニングムービーから、ブルーを基調色にしたシンプルでポップなインタフェースへの展開が気持ちいい。サイトのデザインはincomingvision。

The official Web site of Colal, a Portuguese clothing brand. The opening movie is speedy with a techno music soundtrack, and it flows comfortably with the blue-hued, simple, and pop main interface. Designed by incomingvision.

Soft ware : A, B-1, B-2, E-4   CL : Colal Lda.   DF : Incomingvision

Id society

http://www.idsociety.com/index_02.html

   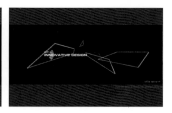

  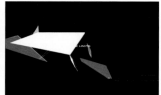 

インタラクティブデザイン／Interactive Design Firm **USA**

インタラクティブデザインを手掛ける「ID Society」のサイト。ガラスの破片のようなエッジの効いた図形が宇宙空間をはじけるイメージか？動くスピードに緩急があり、モーションの流れにメリハリをつけている。

Site for an interactive design company called ID Society. How can the shard-like shapes float over the screen, defying gravity? The transitions fluctuate between slow and rapid, juxtaposing feelings of "ease" and "severity" to accent the flow of motion.

| Soft ware : A | CL : ID Society | DF : ID Society |

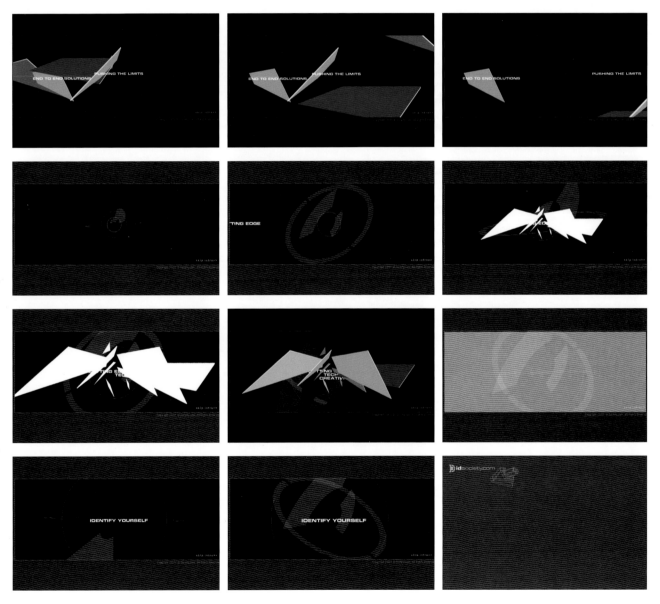

HARD CANDY

http://www.hardcandy.com

女性化粧品／Women's Cosmetics　USA

日本でも大人気のキュートなコスメブランド「HARD CANDY」。シンプルながらセンスを感じさせるデザインで、ブランドイメージをしっかり表現している。プロダクトの紹介も充実しているので、ニューアイテムのチェックには欠かすことのできないサイトだ。

"Hard Candy" is a cute cosmetic brand that is very popular in Japan. The site design is simple, showing good sensibilities by clearly expressing the brand image. Filled with detailed product information, the site is indispensable for checking new items.

Soft ware : A	CL : Hard Candy	DF : ID Society

INDEX

INDEX

Index of Clients

INDEX

Index of Submittors

INDEX

Index of URL

Jacket Design
世浪　淳　Jun Yonami

Designer
アサリ グラフィックス　Asari Graphics

Editor
大桶　真（パブロフ）　OOOKE Makoto(pavlov)

Coordinator
高橋かおる　Kaoru Takahashi

Creative Director
世浪　淳　Jun Yonami

Authoring
外河宏師　Hiroshi Togawa
カセット・エンジニアリング　cassette engineering co.

Translator
Douglas Allsopp
野口世津子　Setsuko Noguchi

Publisher
三芳伸吾　Shingo Miyoshi

WEB Motion Design

WEB モーション デザイン

2002年3月12日初版第1刷発行

発行所　　ピエ・ブックス
〒170-0003 東京都豊島区駒込4-14-6　#301
編集TEL : 03-3949-5010 FAX:03-3949-5650
営業TEL : 03-3940-8302 FAX:03-3576-7361
e-mail : editor@piebooks.com
　　　　 sales@piebooks.com
http://www.piebooks.com

CD-ROMプレス：富士フィルム アクシア（株）
印刷・製本 ：（株）サンニチ印刷

© 2002 by P・I・E BOOKS

ISBN4-89444-188-8 C3070

Printed in Japan
本書の収録内容の無断転載、複写、引用等を禁じます。
落丁、乱丁はお取り替え致します。